9

)0

CLASSIC TRAMCARS

CLASSIC
TRAMCARS

R.J.S.WISEMAN

LONDON

IAN ALLAN LTD

Acknowledgements

The initial impetus for *Classic Tramcars* came from John Price at a meeting in London, late in 1983, when he suggested that I might be interested in tackling the subject as a sequel to *Classic Buses* by Gavin Booth, published a few years earlier.

The writing of this book would have been impossible without the help of my friends and fellow enthusiasts in the tramway field who have offered advice and encouragement throughout the project.

My particular thanks must go, first of all, to Roy Brook who not only provided a vast amount of information but was also kind enough to read through large sections of the manuscript and suggest alterations and improvements which have been incorporated in the text.

The following people have similarly read through the more specialised parts of the book and have provided additional information, made corrections and have helped in many ways: G. E. Baddeley, R. T. Coxon, C. S. Dunbar, R. Elliott, N. N. Forbes, T. S. Golding, F. J. Groves, C. C. Hall, G. S. Hearse, J. B. Horne, D. L. G. Hunter, J. S. King, J. M. Maybin, E. R. Oakley, F. K. Pearson, C. S. Smeeton, I. G. McM. Stewart, A. K. Terry, J. S. Webb, I. A. Yearsley, and finally to John Price for his help at all times during the writing of this book.

I must thank all those named above, and also A. W. Brotchie, W. A. Camwell, and H. B. Priestley for help in the location and, in most cases, the loan of suitable photographs. I further thank all those who are duly acknowledged in the text for permission to use their photographs and also wish to place on record the efforts of Bill Tuckwell and my brother Jeremy in producing prints, often at short notice, for use in this book. Unfortunately, due to lack of space, it has not been possible to use them all in this volume.

Finally it remains for me to thank my wife for her patience, help and encouragement over the last two years during which time the office tended to expand, first to the dining room table, and later over most of the available chairs, and even the floor! Even so I have been allowed to use her photograph of Sheffield 200 among the illustrations.

My thanks to all who have assisted in any way and whose name may have been, inadvertently, missed from the above lists.

First published 1986
Reprinted 1993

ISBN 0 7110 1560 0

Published by Ian Allan Ltd, Shepperton, Surrey; and printed in Great Britain by Ian Allan Printing Ltd, Coombelands House, Addlestone, Surrey KT15 1HY

**All photos are by the author unless otherwise credited.
The line drawings were kindly supplied by E. Thornton and I. G. McM. Stewart.**

Previous page:
Brush-built 'Rocker Panel' No 385 of 1921 passing 1926 standard car No 245 in Fargate, Sheffield, on 19 April 1953.

Contents

Preface

The tramcar had ceased to dominate the urban scene by the time my interest in this vehicle had been aroused. I had spent my early years either abroad or in the countryside far from such scenes. It was only after one of the infrequent visits by the family to relatives in Nottingham when I discovered that the tramcars were no longer running there that my life-long interest began.

I did most of my tramcar travelling in the years between 1944 and 1955 when the choice of vehicle, although diminishing annually, spanned over 50 years of development. It was still possible to travel to the terminus in a wooden tramcar creaking at the joints and return to town in the comfort of a warm, bright interior on an upholstered seat.

In this book I have picked out the tramcars which to me epitomise a vehicle that was the mainstay of public transport for over half a century. To this end I have chosen those cars which illustrate the main advances in design as developed by the major car building firms. In addition the large undertakings, particularly the municipal operators, evolved their own classic designs, and these are also described. To complete the range a final chapter examines seven tramcars with classic status which escaped the breaker's torch and are now preserved at operating museums.

I have also included a number of experimental or prototype cars which were to have formed the base for replacement fleets that were never built.

Although, in most cases, it was the bodywork which gave the tramcar its classic status, it must be remembered that it was the advances in truck and motor design which enabled new body styles to develop.

In the descriptions that follow I have kept technical detail to a minimum and for easy reference standardised tables and line drawings have been given for most of the classic tramcars described.

Right:
Southampton tramcar No 45, the first to be privately preserved, is seen on passenger duty at the National Tramway Museum, Crich, Derbyshire. The facade of the Derby Assembly Rooms is on the left.

Notes on Information

Tramcar builders
The companies named in this book had works in the following locations; this location is given at the head of the tables following the operator's name and number or class of car.

Preston Dick Kerr Works. Electric Railway & Tramway Carriage Works (ER&TCW) 1899-1904; United Electric Car Co (UEC) 1905-1920; English Electric Co (EE) 1920-1940.
Loughborough Falcon Works. Brush Electrical Engineering Co. 1889-1937.
Birkenhead G. F. Milnes 1886-1904; G. C. Milnes Voss & Co 1906-1910.
Hadley G. F. Milnes 1900-1904.
Motherwell Hurst Nelson & Co Ltd (HN) 1899-1935.
Trafford Park British Electric Car Co (BEC) 1901-1904.

Tramcars were also built by some other companies, ie, Cravens of Darnall, Sheffield, Charles Roberts of Horbury (both as indicated in the text), and also, often on a large scale, in the workshops of the municipal and some company undertakings.

Stairs
The three basic type of staircase used in tramcar construction were:
Normal A spiral staircase turning anti-clockwise from the platform.
Reversed A spiral staircase turning clockwise from the platform.
These stairs were usually of quarter-turn (90°) or half-turn (180°) type.
Broken or Landing A two-part staircase with a landing halfway.
Straight A staircase leading directly from the platform, in most cases with a quarter turn at the platform end.

Seating
In the lower saloon, transverse seating generally included two longitudinal seats, each for two passengers, over the sandboxes at each end of the saloon. On the upper deck transverse seating includes balcony seats where appropriate. 2+2 indicates rows of double seats, and 2+1 one double and one single row. Abbreviations: T – Transverse; W – Wooden; L – Longitudinal; U – Upholstered.

Trucks
Four-wheeled or single trucks with wheelbase and wheel diameter. Eight-wheeled or bogie trucks with wheelbase and wheel diameter.

Bogie trucks were of two basic types; equal-wheeled or maximum traction (MaxT) with one larger driving wheel and pony wheel. In some cases the trucks were reversed with the pony wheels at the outer ends of the car.

The main truck types were: Brill, and Peckham, originating in the United States and manufactured later under licence in Britain. Later designs were developed by the Electro-Mechanical Brake Co, and Maley & Taunton Ltd of Wednesbury.

Motors
Two or four motor equipments, usually indicated in the form 2 × BTH 509; 50hp.

Controllers
One on each platform in the form BTH B.510. Name and type.

Brakes
All tramcars had a hand brake working on the wheels. Braking was also on the track (slipper brake). Rheostatic braking and magnetic braking was available and later cars were fitted with various types of air brake.

Gauge: Given only when non-standard.

Note: In a few cases two sets of dimensions are given for one entry. This indicates that sources disagree on the data.

1. The Development of the Tramcar

To-day transport of both passengers and goods is taken for granted, and the development of the various modes has led to the growth of large urban areas extending for many miles into the surrounding countryside.

Two hundred years ago the majority of West Europeans lived in small communities and their movements were very limited, with few people venturing beyond the village fields and the nearby market town. This was to change little during the early days of industrial expansion. Industry needs a power source and, until the coming of oil and electricity, had to be located at a water power site or on a coalfield. The labour requirement was high and the workforce had to live in close proximity to the foundry, workshop or mill, and so tightly packed communities grew up on the coalfields which fuelled the industrial development of the 19th century.

Industrial expansion was also made possible, and indeed accelerated, by the development of the railways which transported not only the materials required but also the workers over increasing distances. The railway, however, was limited in scope, as passengers boarded and alighted at stations some distance apart and often remote from the housing areas.

The problem of inconvenient stations was overcome by the development of transport along the public roads. Horse drawn buses and trams had the advantage over the railway of bringing their vehicles to the front doors of the houses and to the

Cable car – No 208, built by Brown Marshall, photographed after its take-over by Edinburgh Corporation in 1919.
E. O. Catford courtesy D. L. G. Hunter

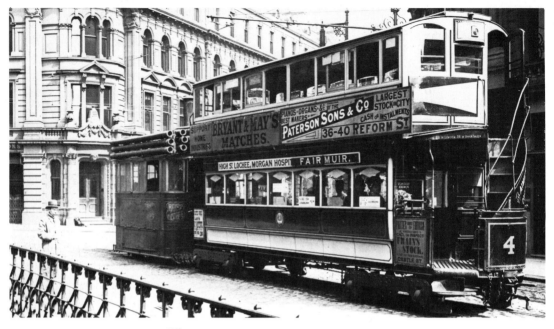

gates of the factories. The tram, moreover, had the advantage over the bus of running on rails which gave less resistance than the uneven cobbled roads, and allowed smoother travel, quicker acceleration and less effort for the horses.

The first tramway was opened in 1860 at Birkenhead by an American, George Francis Train, and the cars for this and many subsequent lines were imported from the United States of America. However a few years later his manager, George Starbuck, set up a works in Birkenhead which built over 800 tramcars during the horse tramway 'boom' of 1875-85.

Steam tram – The large bogie tramcar was popular with steam tramway operators. No 4 built for the Dundee & District Tramways Co Ltd is seen under Corporation ownership. It seated 66 passengers (28 LW/38 TW) and ran until 1902. The engine was built by Green in 1894. *N. B. Traction collection*

Horse drawn tramcars were slow, relatively expensive to operate and required large studs of horses, and it was not surprising that engineers looked for alternative methods of traction. Steam tram engines enjoyed 20 years of success (1880-1900), and cable trams were used where

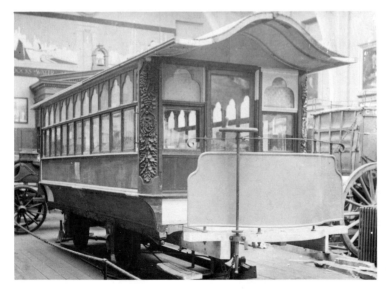

Horse tram – The Ryde Pier tramcar of 1871 has been preserved at the Hull Transport Museum since 1936. Numerous window pillars and the turtle-back roof were features of the earliest designs. *courtesy J. H. Price*

gradients were steep as in Edinburgh, but after numerous experiments – eg the Dolter stud system – electric traction with overhead current collection became dominant from 1900 onwards.

The evolution of the British tramcar spans almost a century, and electric tramcar construction can be divided into four distinct periods – 1883-93 Experimental; 1893-1902 American; 1903-30 Traditional; and 1931-61 Modern. (Based on the Museum of British Transport classification: *Tramcars;* J. H. Price, Veteran & Vintage series, Ian Allan Ltd 1963).

Before examining the classic designs it is

Traditional construction methods

Above:
The Lanarkshire Tramways Co rebuilt tramcar No 31 (Brush 1904) and others in about 1922. The picture shows constructional details of bulkheads, rocker panels, window pillars and the workmanship needed to produce a robust tramcar. *N. B. Traction collection*

worthwhile considering the factors determining the design from both the builder and the operators point of view. The builder was constrained by the technical knowledge of the time and the earliest designs were based on established horsebus

The complexity of turtle-back roof construction is seen in this view of Southampton No 45.

practice. The bodies were of wood, the upright members forming the corner and window pillars, and the longitudinal members the waist and cant rails. The early designs had numerous small windows and pillars in order to give the necessary strength to support the roof and upper deck. Cross members were added to form the bulkheads and give strength to the frame. The lower saloon sides were divided longitudinally into two parts, the waist panel and the rocker panel. The latter was a concave panel running the length of the lower saloon body below the waist panel, giving extra width where it was most needed.

In early double-deck vehicles a turtle-back saloon roof supported a knifeboard seat placed lengthwise centrally along the upper deck. Other roof forms included the clerestory and the monitor: the former gave extra headroom in the centre of the car at the cost of a weakened roof, and with time the many joints worked loose and rainwater seeped through into the saloon.

The operators, both municipal and private, aimed at attracting the maximum number of passengers either to relieve the rates or to boost dividends. In the early days of electric tramways speed was not essential; the majority of passengers, accustomed to the speed of the horse, were in no hurry, travelled relatively short distances and looked to a clean vehicle, courteous staff and a reliable service.

The early tramcars were of strong, simple construction, and numerous coats of paint and varnish were applied to the exterior. An army of cleaners kept the cars spotless inside and out, and the platform staff were smartly turned out. High standards of safety were imposed by the government through the tramway and light railway acts, manifested in the Board of Trade 'bullseye' light in the offside bulkhead of the car. Reliability was less easy to achieve in the early days, but the development of new motors, resistances and braking systems rapidly improved the situation as the electric tramcar came to dominate the urban transport scene during the first decades of the present century.

It was during this period of expansion that the traditional British tramcar evolved. To meet the upsurge in demand production methods were standardised and over 2,000 tramcars were produced annually. However, once the existing tramways had been electrified and associated extensions built, the demand for new rolling stock declined, a number of the smaller manufacturers went into liquidation, and by 1905 production was concentrated at United Electric Car Co Ltd (later English Electric) at Preston and the Brush Company at Loughborough. Some smaller or non-specialist firms continued to produce tramcars until the 1930s (Hurst Nelson of Motherwell, and Cravens of Sheffield, for example).

The largest tramway systems were under municipal control. Among these cities Glasgow, Liverpool, Manchester and Sheffield were major tramcar builders, but London and Birmingham, although possessing well-equipped workshops in which they repaired and modernised their rolling stock, built few new tramcars. On the other hand many of the smaller systems built tramcars which were fitted with equipment purchased from outside firms.

Unfortunately for the tramcar-building industry most tramway undertakings were content to

The simplified roof construction of the 1899 'Preston' car as supplied to Liverpool Corporation.
GEC Traction, courtesy J. B. Horne

SEATS FOR 22 PASSENGERS

Above:
**The Bulkhead of a Liverpool
'Preston' car.** *GEC Traction,
courtesy J. B. Horne*

Left:
**A single-truck, three-window car
with extended canopies. Built at
Hadley in 1902 for the Croydon
District Tramways, No 25 passed to
the SMET in 1906. Similar cars were
supplied to the Bath and South
Lancashire companies. The car
featured Milnes 'Exhibition'
staircases, a single saloon door and
seating for 22 LW/33 TW.**
Real Photographs

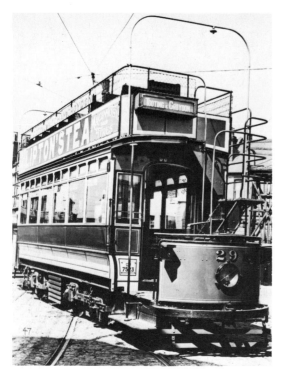 

improve their existing fleets instead of investing in new cars. The visible signs of this were the fitting of top covers and the trend towards the all-enclosed double-deck tramcar. The fitting of top covers allowed the lower saloon roof to be of simpler construction, and vestibules gave more protection from the weather, but the open-top double-decker did not disappear from the urban scene until 1947 when the vestibuled bogie cars of Blackburn Corporation were withdrawn. They were last seen on football duty at Ewood Park, and despite their years were still in excellent condition.

The Llandudno & Colwyn Bay Electric Railway purchased open-top Brush-built bogie cars from Bournemouth Corporation in 1936 and these were still operating when the line closed 20 years later, but this was an exceptional case, the cars being used for summer seaside holiday traffic.

The result of all the 'improvements' to vehicles was a large variation in the looks of the traditional tramcar; for example, by 1924 Huddersfield Corporation's first 70 cars had been rebuilt or modified to produce 15 different designs, and even Southend with a fleet of 40 cars in 1919 could boast 11 different types and sub-types. In many cases the additional weight of the top covers was too much for the original lower saloon structures and these in turn had to be rebuilt or replaced. This would often result in four-window lower saloons supporting three-window top decks or vice-versa. There was also a wide variety of staircase – half turn, quarter

Above left:
A bogie six-window short roof car with broken staircase. Built at Loughborough in 1902 for Croydon District, No 29 also passed to the SMET in 1906. Note narrow bulkhead window and double saloon doors; seating is for 30 LW/39 TW. *Real Photographs*

Above:
A bogie five-window car with reversed stairs. Built at Preston in 1902 for the Gravesend & Northfleet Tramways Co (BET), No 34 was one of four cars transferred to the SMET in 1906-07. Seating is for 34 LW/34 TW. *Real Photographs*

turn, normal turn (clockwise) or reversed (anti-clockwise), as well as the divided or broken staircase with a landing halfway.

All this rebuilding, usually in the municipal workshops, lead to a stagnation in design so that when there was a temporary boom following the end of World War 1 only more refined versions of the traditional tramcar could be offered. Nevertheless, the tramcar enthusiast of this period had a bewildering choice; it was possible to travel for up to 50 miles or more on a succession of local tramcars in London, Birmingham, West Yorkshire, South Lancashire and the Clyde Valley, for example. The tramcars ranged from open-top to all enclosed with every variety in between, not to mention the range of single-deck cars on the many rural lines or where low bridges forbade the use of double-deckers.

Above:
Newcastle Corporation No 212 was built by Brush about 1912 and is a good illustration of the vestibuled open-balcony car of the period. Angular dashes, wide windscreens and reversed stairs were features of these cars. Seating was for 21 TW/34 TW.

Above:
Dundee Corporation electrified the former horse and steam tramways from 13 July 1900 onwards, running short-roof open-top 'Preston' cars of three and five-window designs. No 4 is of the latter type on Perth Road in 1929. It had been top-covered in 1908 and underwent a second metamorphosis in 1930 to emerge as an enclosed car.
N. B. Traction collection

By 1925 or thereabouts the trolleybus and motor omnibus were gaining ground rapidly and tramcar design was stimulated by the growing competition. New motors and new trucks enabled a high capacity 'low bridge' double-decker to be produced: the rocker panel disappeared, platform doors were fitted, seats were upholstered, lighting improved and the new equipment gave rapid acceleration and higher speeds.

By 1932 modern tramcars were available, but unfortunately there was little demand and most new cars were built in the municipal workshops in Glasgow, Liverpool and Sheffield. New methods of construction, especially the use of metal alloys, enabled the angular outlines of the traditional tramcar to be modified, and many pleasing designs were to be seen on the streets up to the end of city tramway operation in 1962.

Tramcar design in Britain almost came to an end when modern single-deck railcars were built for Blackpool by Charles Roberts of Horbury, and for Leeds by C. H. Roe of Crossgates, but in 1984 a new single-deck tramcar appeared on the promenade at Blackpool.

Above:
Newcastle's well-equipped Byker works built tramcars from 1903 onwards. These included the enclosed 'B' class cars Nos 240-309. No 266, built in 1922, is seen here outside the central station. Features included front exits, airbrakes and Peckham P22 trucks.

Below:
Manchester was the hub of a large network extending well beyond the city boundaries – Manchester Exchange was the terminus for routes to Hyde, Stockport and Hazel Grove. Stockport No 58, an English Electric car of 1921, waits for a Manchester bogie car to cross over. *W. A. Camwell*

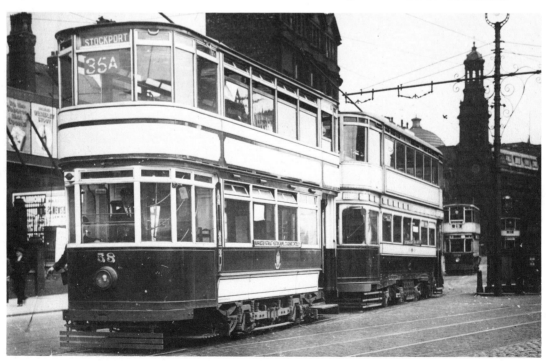

2. Standard Designs

Dick Kerr, Preston

The expansion and electrification of tramways caused a rapid acceleration in the demand for tramcars from 1899 onwards, and while the old established firms remained prosperous, Dick Kerr & Co, general engineers of Kilmarnock, was the most successful. The company had workshops in Preston, and in 1898 formed a subsidiary company, The Electric Railway & Tramway Carriage Works Ltd, to build tramcars, and a second, The English Electric Manufacturing Co, to supply the electrical equipment which at that time was imported from the United States of America.

The new car works opened in 1899 under the able management of E. A. Stanley who introduced the new flow methods of construction and a new design of tramcar. This new design included the almost flat lower saloon roof in place of the monitor style which had been inherited from the horse car builders. The first 'Preston' standard cars had a three-window saloon with opening lights above, and these, together with the new roof form, gave a more spacious saloon with more room, light and air. Longitudinal benches down each side seated a total of 22 passengers. This design, known as the short roof design retained the short canopy over the platform from which quarter turn stairs led directly to the open-top deck on which rows of transverse 'garden seats' accommodated up to 30 more passengers. These cars had imported Brill 21E trucks and equipment.

Tramcars of this design were supplied to Liverpool, Bolton, Oldham and Dundee among others, as well as to companies in the British Electric Traction group; however, within a year the

The earliest 'Preston' design had a short roof and direct stairs. Bolton was an early customer with an order for 40 cars in 1899.
Real Photographs

17

A typical 'Preston' 1901 type double-deck car with reversed stair. *E. Thornton*

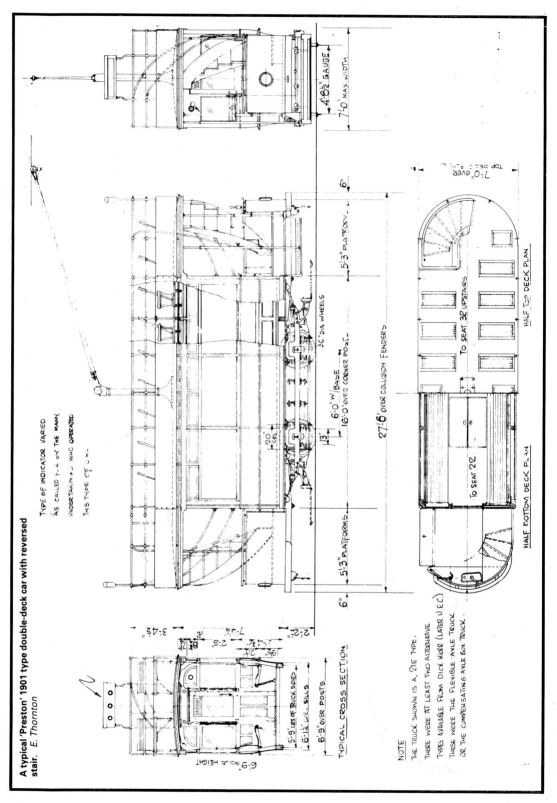

TYPE OF INDICATOR VARIED AS CALLED FOR BY THE MANY UNDERTAKINGS WHO OPERATED THIS TYPE OF CAR.

4·8½" GAUGE

7'-0" MAX. WIDTH

6"

5'-3" PLATFORM

30" DIA. WHEELS

6'-0" W/BASE

16'-0" OVER CORNER POST

20" CRS.

13"

27'-6" OVER COLLISION FENDERS

5'-3" PLATFORMS

6"

7'-0" OVER TOP DECK FLOOR

HALF TOP DECK PLAN

TO SEAT 30 UPSTAIRS

HALF BOTTOM DECK PLAN

TO SEAT 22

3'-4½"

7'-9¾"

2'-6"

1'-4¾"

1'-6½"

8'-7½"

2'-7¼"

6'-9" INSIDE HEIGHT

5'-9" CRS OF TRUCK SIDES

6'-1¼" WE. SILLS

6'-9" OVER POSTS

TYPICAL CROSS SECTION

NOTE

THE TRUCK SHOWN IS A. 21E TYPE.
THERE WERE AT LEAST TWO ALTERNATIVE
TYPES AVAILABLE FROM DICK KERR (LATER U EC.)
THESE WERE THE FLEXIBLE 'AXLE TRUCK
OR THE COMPENSATING AXLE BOX TRUCK.

18

short roof design was obsolete, although the last vehicles to be built at Preston were delivered to Cardiff as late as 1902.

The short roof design of 1899 only seated a maximum of 52 passengers and offered little protection from the weather to the crew, so it is hardly surprising that the next advance was to extend the canopies to the full length of the car. To fully utilise the extra space now available the quarter turn (90°) reversed stair was introduced, and the curved seats on the canopy increased the seating capacity to 56 (23+34), or even 76 (30+46) on the longer bogie cars.

This type of car was developed by C. R. Bellamy, the Liverpool Corporation Tramways manager, who also incorporated the reversed stair as a safety feature: passengers ascending and descending while the car was in motion would not be thrown off the car and would therefore use the stairs with the car moving; hence a faster service.

The Preston works started delivering these cars to Liverpool in March 1900 and by the end of 1901, 300 had arrived. To deliver that number of cars in 19 months, in addition to hundreds of similar cars for systems throughout the British Isles, was a real achievement.

The importance of the new 'Liverpool car' as it was known at the time can be illustrated by the fact that at least three undertakings – Portsmouth, Bolton and Oldham – changed their orders from the short-roof type to the new improved type with extended canopies and reversed stairs. Portsmouth Corporation purchased 80 of these cars at an extra cost of £40 per car. The body frame was of pitch pine and oak, the interior woodwork quartered oak, and over the three side windows there was a fine cornice of embossed mouldings. All panel work in doors and bulkheads was moulded with embossed beading, and metal furnishings were polished brass.

These trams, however, were still open-top, and Mr Bellamy, ever anxious to improve comfort and to increase revenue, first experimented with top covers in 1902. His first covers were lightly built

The extended canopy car with reversed stairs was built in large numbers. Portsmouth No 12, one of 80 supplied in 1901-04, is seen in its later years. *W. J. Haynes*

with canvas screens which could be rolled up when not required. The covers were supported by glazed bulkheads clear of the stairs and leaving the balcony unroofed. On the open cars the trolley mast was fixed to the floor, but the centre portion of the new roof now supported the trolley base, and the extra space provided could be used for seating. The capacity of the car was now 64:22 in the lower saloon as before, 36 on the top deck and three on the curved seat of each balcony.

The canvas blinds were not really practical, especially in stormy weather, and from 1903 the covers were glazed and the roofs fitted with sliding panels in place of the canvas. These, however, were expensive to maintain and from 1905 onwards were replaced by permanent roofs. The standard car in Liverpool, therefore, had a three-window saloon, a longer five-window upper saloon, 90° reversed stairs, and open, unroofed balconies above the unvestibuled platforms. Liverpool continued to build similar cars at Lambeth Road until 1913.

Meanwhile in 1903 the Dick Kerr works had introduced the full-length top cover with open balconies and the 180° reversed stair which had been successfully introduced by the British Electric Car Co. Probably the first cars of this type were supplied to Bolton Corporation (Nos 82-86). These had the standard 16ft body and seated 56 passengers (22+34). The extra revenue generated by the new top covers effectively made open-top cars outdated except where circumstances dictated otherwise, and the canopied open balcony car became the standard product of the Preston works for the next two decades.

By 1905 the demand for tramcars had declined and in that year the United Electric Car Co was formed by amalgamating the Electric Railway & Tramway Carriage works with the English Electric

Portsmouth Corporation Tramways Nos 1-80
Built: Preston 1901-04
Length overall: – 27ft 10in
Length over corner posts: – 16ft 0in
Length of platforms: – 5ft 3in
Width overall: – 6ft 10½in
Width over corner posts: – 6ft 9in
Height inside lower saloon: – 6ft 6in
Stairs: – Reversed 90°
Seats (lower saloon): – 22 LW
Seats (upper saloon): – 33 TW 2+2
Trucks: – Brill 21E; 6ft wheelbase
Motors: – 2 x DK; 25hp
Brakes: – Peacock hand wheel, rheostatic
Gauge: – 4ft 7¾in

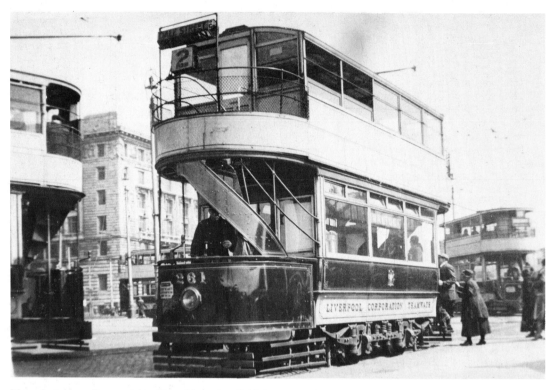

Manufacturing Co, and by absorbing the British Electric Car Co and G. F. Milnes (which had failed in 1904). Tramcar production was now concentrated at Preston, and the works of the other companies were closed down and eventually sold.

Also in 1905 the company produced what was to become its final standard tramcar body. The new three-window design had four air scoops on the cant rail and direct 180° spiral stairs, although cars with air scoops and reversed stairs were supplied to Newport Corporation (Nos 31-40 in 1905 and Nos 42-44 in 1909), and six other customers.

The new standard car proved popular and purchasers included Birmingham, Stockport and Darlington Corporations. It should be noted that the Birmingham cars were supplied with open-top decks, but those to Stockport in 1906-07 and the two to Darlington in 1913 were open balcony cars.

The company also produced a single-truck tramcar with a body longer than the standard 16ft; this had four side windows, and systems supplied included Birmingham Corporation and the Dunfermline & District Tramways Co.

The standard body for bogie cars also had four side windows: the earlier design was supplied to Bolton Corporation (Nos 60-81) in 1901-02; and 20 open-top cars of the later design, with the four air scoops but with reversed stairs, opened the Birmingham Corporation Tramways in 1904. All later bogie cars had normal spiral stairs.

Liverpool was Preston's best customer for the open-top reversed stair tramcar. They were later fitted with Bellamy top-covers. No 261, seen here at the Pier Head, has the hexagonal destination indicator which was standard equipment on these cars. *M. J. O'Connor*

Darlington Corporation Tramways Nos 17-18.
Built: Preston 1913
Length overall: – 28ft 6in
Length over corner posts: – 16ft 0in
Width overall: – 6ft 6in
Width over corner posts: – 6ft 2½in
Height to trolley plank: – 14ft 11¾in
Height inside lower saloon: – 6ft 0in
Height inside upper saloon: – 5ft 8in
Stairs: – Direct 180°
Seats (lower saloon): – 22 LW
Seats (upper saloon): – 33 TW 2+2
Trucks: – Preston flexible axle; 8ft wheelbase; 31¾in diameter wheels
Motors: – Siemens
Controllers: – Siemens
Brakes: – Hand wheel, rheostatic
Gauge: – 3ft 6in

In 1920 the United Electric Car Co, in its turn, became part of the newly formed English Electric Co, and the Preston works turned out its final design of traditional tramcar. In its ultimate form the car was fully enclosed with a three or-four-window body and the four air scoops. The largest order was from Leeds Corporation for 75 car bodies (Nos 76-150).

Below:

The short-roof design was obsolete by 1902 when Cardiff Corporation took delivery of its initial fleet from Preston. No 11 (*Below* **) of the series 1-20, 55-74, is shown at Clive Road terminus. Clearly visible are the folding gate closed across the driver's platform and the 'broken' staircase specified for these particular cars. These features are also shown on the bogie car (** *Bottom* **). Nos 21-40 and 75-94 were delivered at the same time and had Brill maximum traction bogies.**
Both courtesy H. B. Priestley

The last orders came from the smaller concerns either as replacements for older cars scrapped or to meet the needs of short extensions. It is probable that the last open-top cars to the traditional three-window design were supplied to Dover Corporation in 1920 (Nos 25-27), although the last open-top cars were Plymouth Corporation bogie cars Nos 131-150 delivered in 1924.

Enclosed cars built included Oldham Corporation Nos 121-132 in 1926 and Nottingham Corporation Nos 181-200 in 1926-27. These latter were probably the last single-truck cars built at Preston to the traditional design, but balcony top covers were being supplied as late as 1930 to Rochdale Corporation, and four-window enclosed bogie cars to Bolton in 1927-28 (Nos 139-150; 104-106).

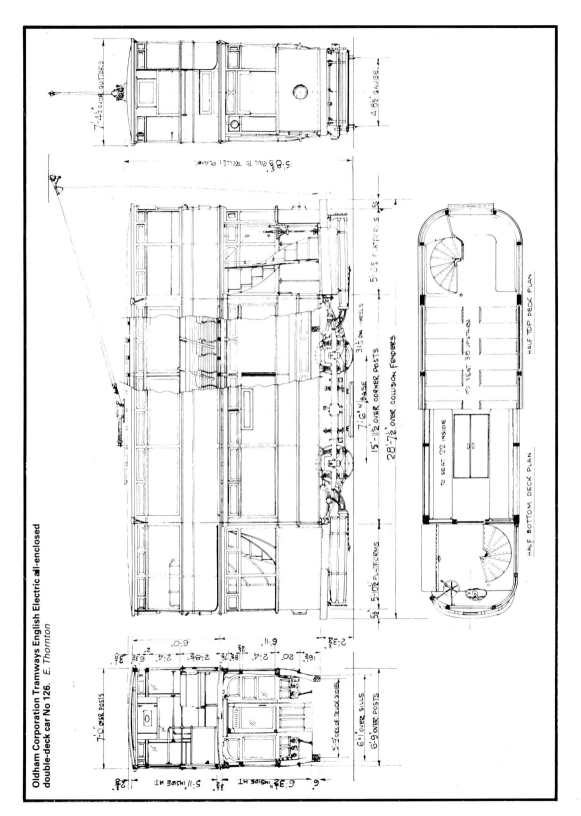

Oldham Corporation Tramways English Electric all-enclosed double-deck car No 126. *E. Thornton*

7' 4½" OVER GUTTERS

4.8½" GAUGE

15'8½" RAIL TO TROLLEY PLANK.

5½" PLATFORMS

5½" FLATRIBBOLS

3'1" DIA. WHEELS

7'6" W/BASE

15'1½" OVER CORNER POSTS

28'7½" OVER COLLISION FENDERS

5'0½" PLATFORMS

5½" PLATFORMS

HALF TOP DECK PLAN

TO SEAT 38 UPSTAIRS

TO SEAT 22 INSIDE

HALF BOTTOM DECK PLAN

7'0" OVER POSTS

6'0"

6'11"

2'5¾"

1'6¾" 2'0" 2'4" 2'8½" 3'½" 2'4" 6'3¾" 3'¾"

6'1" OVER TRUCK SIDES

6'9" OVER POSTS

6'1" OVER SILLS

5'0" OVER TRUCK SIDES

2'8"

6'3½" 3'¾" 5'-11" INSIDE HT 3'¾" 6' 5'-11" INSIDE HT 2'8"

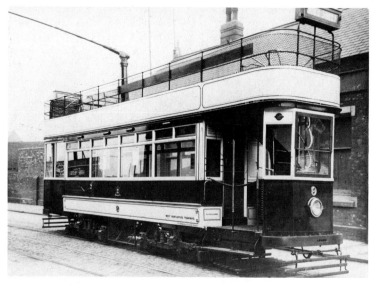

Traditional open-top tramcars were built at Preston until 1924: the last were single-truck cars Nos 131-150 for Plymouth Corporation. A year earlier two open-top bogie cars were supplied to West Hartlepool Corporation. The third car was numbered 9, had the Brill 22E bogies from the previous No 9 and incorporated all the features of the 1905 design. *G. E. C. Traction*

The end of the traditional line

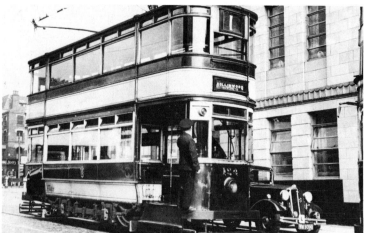

Left:
Oldham No 126 was built at Preston in 1926 and was photographed in Oldham Market Place on 2 August 1938. *H. B. Priestley*

Below left:
Bogie cars for Bolton were the last, and No 144 of 1927 on Brush 22E bogies exhibits all the classic Preston features.
Real Photographs

Brush

The Brush Company of Loughborough was the second largest producer of electric tramcars in Great Britain. The company could trace its history back to 1897, although the Brush Electrical Engineering Co was not registered until 10 August 1899, when the new firm purchased the Falcon Engine & Car Works which had been building steam tram engines and trailers since 1885.

The earliest orders for double-deck electric tramcars came in 1895 from Guernsey, Norwich, Coventry and the Douglas Southern, the three latter systems being constructed by the New General Traction Co. The tramcars for these lines were all craftsman-built, about three weeks being needed for each car. The first five Coventry cars were typical of the experimental period of construction and were simply double-deck versions of the large order Brush was fulfilling for Rouen at this time. The six-window bodies were similar in many ways to the steam tram trailers constructed 10 years previously at the same works for the Coventry-Bedworth line. The bodies were of the short-roof type with the turtle-back roof profile and open-top decks. The saloon had longitudinal benches seating 20 passengers, while the knifeboard seat above, astride the lower saloon roof as it were, seated another 20. Decency panels and railings protected the passengers on the top deck, which was reached by a curved staircase from the middle of each platform. The driver's only protection from the weather was the front dash, there being the passenger entrance on the nearside and a metal grill up to the corner posts behind the stairs. The cars had Peckham Cantilever trucks, two Westinghouse 27hp motors and Westinghouse 28A controllers, all from the USA.

When a further 10 cars were supplied in 1899 the saloon had been re-designed to some extent; it now had five side windows with curved tops, and garden seats on the top deck. Curved tops to the saloon windows were a characteristic feature of the early tramcars, both double- and single-deck, which were by now being supplied in substantial numbers to the fast growing companies controlled by the British Electric Traction Co (BET), a company with which Brush was closely associated. As BET controlled nearly 40 tramways, and as Brush supplied most of the tramcars required, they were to be seen throughout the country.

The Douglas Southern cars – six motors (Nos 1-6) and six trailers (Nos 7-12) – were delivered in 1896. Nos 7 and 8 were motorised the following year and new trailers Nos 13-16 purchased: they were open-top, open-sided double-deck cars with short roofs and quarter-turn stairs. They had solid bulkheads with a bench seat facing forward and could be described as open-top toast-racks with garden seats above.

The Douglas Southern tramway was built on the landward side of the Marine Drive, a spectacular private road which linked Douglas Head with Port Soderick, some four miles to the south. As the trams were never turned, both staircases faced the

---

Douglas Head Marine Drive Ltd Nos 1-6
Built: Loughborough 1896
Length overall: – 26ft 2in/28ft 4in
Width overall: – 7ft 4in
Height to trolley plank: – 15ft 6in/14ft 4in
Stairs: – Direct 90°; both on same side of car
Seats (lower saloon): – 36 LW
Seats (upper saloon(: – 39 LW
Trucks: – Lord Baltimore equal-wheel bogies; 6ft 6in wheelbase; 33in diameter wheels
Motors: – 2 x Westinghouse 12A; 25hp
Controllers: – Westinghouse 28A
Brakes: – Hand wheel, electric via controller and canopy switch

---

Below:
Douglas Southern No 4 was built by Brush in 1896 for a line that operated during the summer only. The car is seen at Rebog looking northeast towards Douglas. Construction details visible include glazed bulkheads, garden seats on top, the trolley standard on the landward and stairs down to the seaward side of the car.
B. Y. Williams, courtesy F. K. Pearson

sea and the trolley standard was on the landward side; the overhead was supported by bracket arms and the poles were also on the landward side.

The trams were built with running boards on both sides, although in normal operation only the seaward side was used and a moveable barrier rail was fitted across the landward side. Four cars, Nos 1-3 and 6, were later modified to allow access on the seaward side only. The livery was an attractive crimson and white lined out in gold and white. The destination 'Port Soderick' was painted on the curved panels, above the short roof, at each end of the car.

These cars with seats for 75 passengers were built for a coastal tramway operating during the summer months only and so could hardly be described as standard tramcars, but they were built before the mass production era; No 1, now at the National Tramway Museum at Crich, can surely be described as a classic tramcar.

In 1898 the Brush Co set out to build complete tramcars, and its new works at Loughborough (covering nearly five acres of ground) was completed within two years. The works, like that at Preston, was laid out for flow production, with the body shop capable of turning out up to 750 cars a year. The company could also supply the necessary electrical equipment, motors and trucks, and claimed to be the first firm to build an all-British tramcar.

The new works was ready just in time to meet the expanding demand and offered a range of 10 standard cars which, it said, would meet every operating requirement. The body design was still based on the monitor roof, and large numbers were sold to Manchester, Leeds and Bradford

Corporations, as well as to BET companies. Although the simpler roof construction was introduced in 1902 – and from then on this became the standard Brush tramcar – the monitor roof was still preferred by Manchester among others. The elegance of this roof and civic pride may have been the reasons why it was able to compete with the cheaper products then available.

Bournemouth Corporation's fleet of over 100 open-top cars, excluding the 16 acquired from Poole & District in 1905, were all to the monitor roof design, and the last examples were supplied by Brush as late as 1926. It was certainly outdated by this time, but the narrow gauge track and the limited loading gauge prevented the use of covered top decks or wider bodies with transverse upholstered seats in the lower saloon. The last 20 cars, Nos 113-132, had four windows with the classic curved tops and hinged ventilators, only the vestibuled platforms adding a modern touch. Ten of these cars were purchased by the Llandudno & Colwyn Bay Electric Railway when the Bournemouth tramways closed in 1936, and these saw another 20 years service along the North Wales coast. In Llandudno they were painted in a green and cream livery, and as these cars too were never turned the destinations could be painted on the car sides; Llandudno at the western end and Colwyn Bay at the eastern.

Returning to Loughborough, the main features of the Brush 1902 standard design were an almost flat saloon roof, a plain cant rail, flat-topped windows and simple ventilation by opening lights. These cars had extended canopies and direct or reversed stairs. Newcastle Corporation Nos 131-165 were four-window cars with reversed stairs while

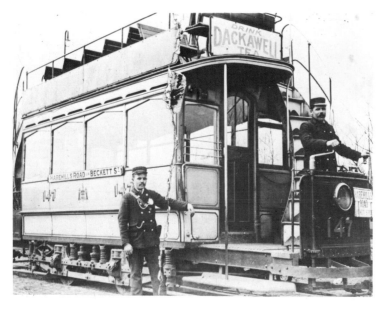

Brush supplied short-roof cars to Leeds and Bradford Corporations. Platform and bulkhead construction is well shown in this view of Leeds No 147, one of 50 built in 1899.
Courtesy R. Brook

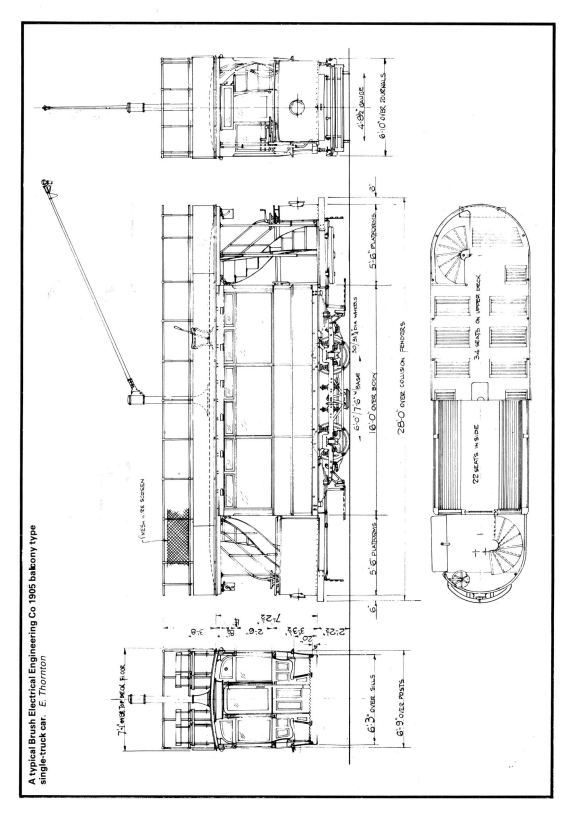

A typical Brush Electrical Engineering Co 1905 balcony type single-truck car. *E. Thornton*

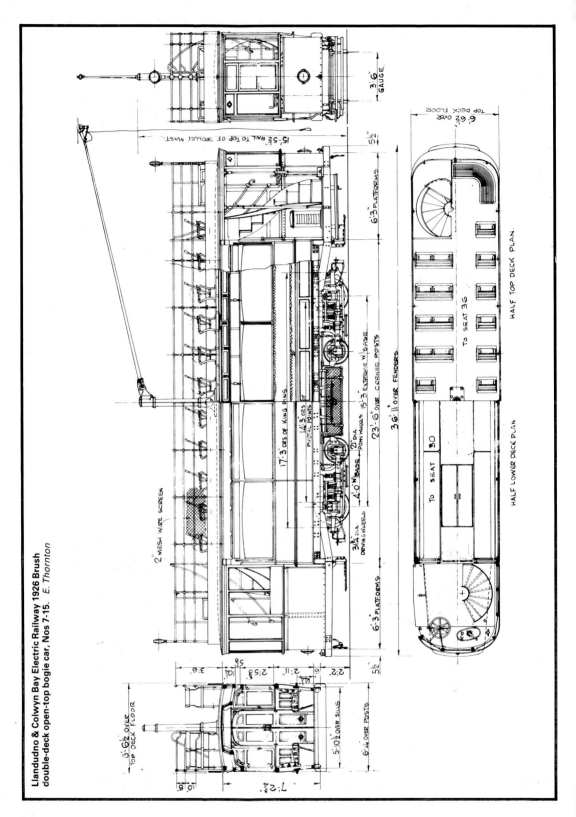

Llandudno & Colwyn Bay Electric Railway 1926 Brush double-deck open-top bogie car, Nos 7-15. *E. Thornton*

28

Barnsley & District (a BET company) Nos 1-12 had three windows and reversed stairs.

The classic Brush open-top car with three side windows, direct spiral stairs and six air scoops appeared in 1905, although Walthamstow Council opened its system in 1904 with cars of this type, but they lacked the looped stair rail which became standard when the general production run started in 1905. The largest customer was Belfast Corporation which ordered 170 cars (Nos 1-170); they became known as 'Standard Reds' and were in service until 1950.

These cars had extended canopies, were oak-framed and were reinforced with steel corner plates. The interior woodwork was oak and mahogany and ceilings bird's eye maple. This design remained in production for almost 30 years in its open top, open-balcony and enclosed forms and, to meet the varied needs of the tramway operators, four- and five-window versions were available as well as longer bodies for bogie vehicles.

Examples included Nottingham Nos 146-155 of 1919, standard gauge open-balcony four-window cars with four air scoops on Peckham P22 trucks; and Accrington Nos 38-41 of 1915 and 1920, 4ft gauge enclosed five-window cars with six air scoops on Brush maximum traction bogies. Nos

Belfast Corporation Tramways Nos 1-170
Built: Loughborough 1905-
Length overall: – 28ft 0in
Length over corner posts: – 16ft 0in
Width overall: – 6ft 10in
Height to top of scrollwork: – 13ft 2½in
Height inside lower saloon: – 6ft 10in
Stairs: – Direct 180°
Seats (lower saloon): – 22 LW slatted
Seats (upper saloon): – 32 TW 2+2
Trucks: – Brill 21E type; 6ft 6in wheelbase
Motors: 2 x Westinghouse 200
Controllers: – British Westinghouse 90N
Brakes: – Hand wheel, rheostatic and slipper

38, 40 and 41 were sold to Southend in 1934, regauged to the narrower 3ft 6in gauge and re-numbered 66-68. No 39 on the other hand was sold to Lytham St Annes and altered to standard gauge as No 55 in that fleet.

A major success for Brush in 1924 was the advent of the low-bridge tramcar. The impetus for

No 181, for the City of Birmingham Tramways Co, photographed outside the Brush works in 1903. On Brush D bogies, it illustrates the 1902 standard car with plain cant rail and ventilation through simple opening lights.
Courtesy J. H. Price

this came from R. L. Horsfield, the manager of the Cardiff Corporation Tramways, where the whole fleet consisted of open-top or single-deck tramcars. The system abounded with low bridges and, as there was little chance of lowering the tram tracks beneath them, Mr Horsfield made tests and found that the overall height of any top-covered car would have to be reduced to under 15ft; that is at least 6in lower than any existing car. In collaboration with the Brush engineers a new top-covered car suitable for Cardiff was designed. The low overall height was made possible by using a well-type underframe, the new smaller motors now available, and 26in diameter wheels. This brought the floor level of the lower saloon to just 25in above rail level: no mean achievement! The four-window body had eight opening ventilators, hinged at one end, and eight air scoops. The interior was spartan; the lower saloon was finished in a highly polished style with longitudinal seating while the upper saloon displayed matchboarding that utilised the polychrome finish of natural polished wood.

The new car, No 101, was a great success and Cardiff purchased a further 80 from Brush, which also received orders from Swansea, Salford and some smaller systems.

Bournemouth Corporation Tramways Nos 113-132
Built: Loughborough 1925-26
Length overall: – 36ft 11in
Length over corner posts: – 23ft 6in
Length of platforms: – 6ft 3in
Width overall: – 6ft 6½in
Width over corner posts: – 6ft 4in
Height to trolley plank: – 15ft 5½in
Height inside lower saloon: – 6ft 7in
Stairs: – Direct 180°
Seats (lower saloon): – 30 LU
Seats (upper saloon): – 36 TW 2+1
Trucks: – Brill 22e MaxT bogies
Motors: – 2 x BTH GE249
Controllers: – MV or BTH B49C
Brakes: – Hand wheel, hand track and magnetic
Gauge: – 3ft 6in

Newcastle Corporation Nos 131-165 were also of the 1902 Brush design with extended canopies and reversed stairs. On a Brill 21E truck, No 160 is seen at Gosforth, probably in 1904. *Courtesy R. Brook*

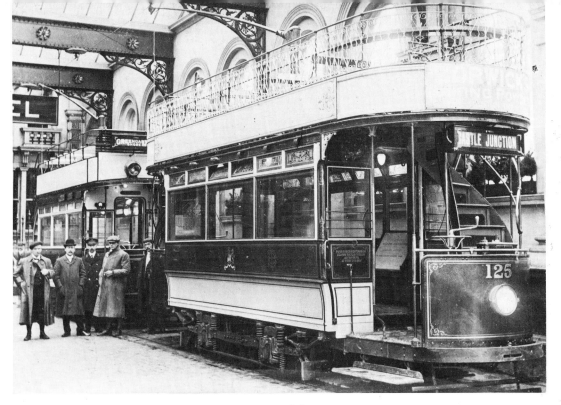

Above:
The 'classic' Brush design of 1905 with six air scoops is seen in Belfast No 125 at the Northern Counties station just prior to the Board of Trade inspection of 29 November 1905. Note the advertisements on the glass ventilator panels. The car behind is a converted horse car. *Courtesy P. M. Maybin*

Below:
Bournemouth Corporation tramcars were nearly all long open-top bogie cars with internal monitor ceilings. No 75 from Brush in 1907 shows the ventilator and window design which was characteristic of these cars. *Courtesy J. H. Price*

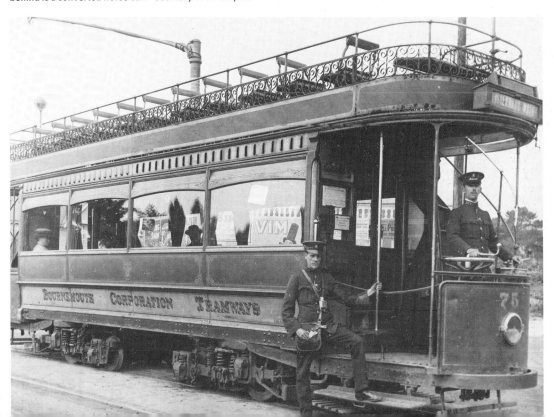

Below:
The Brush Belfast standard cars were fitted with balcony top-covers in the course of time and 50 were further rebuilt as enclosed cars in 1929-32. Belfast covers were of a distinctive design as seen in No 14 in the Donegall Road on 1 July 1939. *W A Camwell*

Bottom:
The Brush lowbridge car with floor level only 25in above rail level was a major success for the company. These cars seated 64 passengers (24 LW/40 TW, 2+2) and had Peckham P22 trucks of 7ft 6in wheelbase. No 25 is seen at Roath Park on 11 April 1938. *H. B. Priestley*

Traditional tramcars continued to come off the Brush production lines, albeit in small numbers, for some years – the last open-top car for Exeter in 1929, the last open balcony car for Coventry in 1931 and the last unvestibuled car for Ilford Council in 1932. By this time the company was producing buses and trolleybuses, but some modern tramcars were produced in the years up to 1937.

G. F. Milnes

In 1886 the Starbuck works at Birkenhead was taken over by George F. Milnes & Co, and it continued to build tramcars for horse, steam and, within a few years, electric traction. The earliest electric cars supplied were of the usual short roof open-top type. They included Nos 11-14 for Dover Corporation with curved top, five-window saloons in 1898, and Nos 1-10 for Halifax Corporation in the same year. The latter had four window saloons, and a more pronounced curve to their tops. These cars all had Peckham Cantilever type trucks of 5ft 6in wheelbase.

Some of the first electric bogie cars to enter service in England were built at Birkenhead for the Imperial Tramways Co which opened the new tramway linking Middlesborough with Thornaby, Stockton and Norton on 16 July 1898. The 50 cars supplied (Nos 1-50) were to a new design by Mr (later Sir) Clifton Robinson, but still retained the short roof and had six curved-top windows to the saloon.

However, the 'classic' Birkenhead cars of this early period were the 180 short-roof, open-top four-window cars supplied to the Bristol Tramways & Carriage Co Ltd during 1900, which were generally similar to the cars supplied a year or two earlier by the American Car Co. These cars had 'Tudor Arch' windows and a monitor roof with ventilation through louvres, as had all the earlier cars.

I well recall my only ride on a Bristol tramcar, to Ashton Gate in January 1940; the lower saloon, entered by double doors, was rather gloomy and retained the Victorian atmosphere with its veneered ceiling, plush cushioning and curtains at the windows. The bulkheads were used for notices,

Imperial Tramways Co No 2 was one of 50 open-top bogie tramcars built by G. F. Milnes for the opening of the Middlesbrough tramway in 1898. Note the elaborate lining out of the vermilion and white livery, the height of the platform above rail level, primitive lifeguards, scrollwork on the platform and exposed driving position.
Courtesy R. Brook

Bristol Tramways & Carriage Co 1900 Milnes short-roof direct stair car. *E. Thornton*

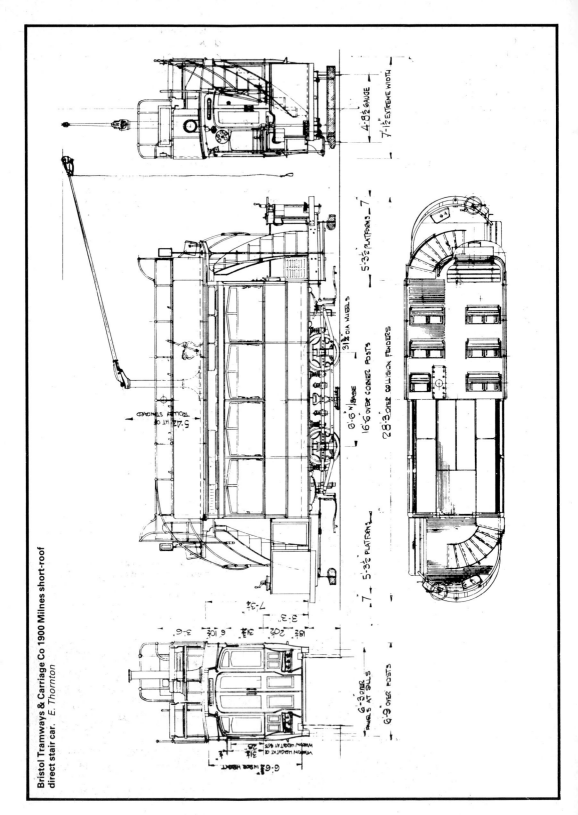

Imperial Tramways Co Ltd, Middlesborough 1-50
Built: Birkenhead 1898
Length overall: – 32ft 4in
Length over corner posts: – 22ft 0in
Length of platforms: – 4ft 8in
Width overall: – 6ft 5½in
Width over corner posts: – 6ft 4in
Height to trolley plank: – 9ft 10½in
Stairs: – Direct 90°
Seats (lower saloon): – 30 LW
Seats (upper saloon): – 30 TW 2+1
Trucks: – Peckham Rev, MaxT bogies; 3ft 6in wheelbase
Motors: – 2 x GE 800; 25-27hp
Controllers: – GE K2B
Brakes: – Hand wheel, and electric emergency
Gauge: – 3ft 7in

including fares on the routes from Bristol Bridge, and the list of colour codes displayed on the cars at night. These were shown by a circular rotating disc by which a different colour could be displayed at the front forward end and the regulation red light at the rear. Unfortunately I did not record the colours used.

The dashes were shallow with ornate scrollwork filling the gap below the direct quarter turn staircase. The headlamp was located above the short canopy, and the livery was an attractive dark blue with gold lining.

The capacity of the Birkenhead works was very limited and in order to meet the expected rush of orders for rolling stock a new works was built on a more spacious site at Hadley, near Wellington, in Shropshire. This opened in 1900 and was very busy during the boom years of 1902-03 with large orders from Manchester, Salford and Bradford. The boom, however, was short lived; the company had over-reached itself and went into liquidation early in 1904. Meantime the Birkenhead works was taken over by George Comer Milnes and Thomas Voss who traded as G. C. Milnes Voss & Co and continued to produce specialised tramcar products including top covers. A limited company, G. C. Milnes Voss & Co Ltd, took over the partnership in 1906.

Blackburn Corporation purchased the local steam tramway companies in 1898 and 1899, rebuilt them for electric traction, and ordered their tramcars from Milnes. The first eight (Nos 28-35) were built at Birkenhead, amd the remaining 40 (Nos 36-75) at Hadley in 1900. These cars illustrate the differences between the 'American' and 'traditional' types of body construction.

Nos 28-35 were open-top short-roof cars with six windows, duplicates of the 50 supplied to Middlesbrough, except that they ran on Brill 22E bogies; canopies and vestibules were added in 1906. The Hadley cars were canopied open-top cars complete with vestibuled platforms. They were probably the only double-deck open-top cars to be built with a level underframe throughout which resulted in the platforms and saloon floor being on the same level without a step. This made it necessary to have a double step from the road to the platform; this is a feature seen on a number of single-deck cars, notably those of the Manx Electric Railway.

Bristol Tramways & Carriage Co Ltd Nos 1-85, 98-115, 119-124, 162-202
Built: Birkenhead 1900
Length overall: – 28ft 3in
Length over corner posts: – 16ft 6in
Length of platforms: – 5ft 3½in
Width overall: – 7ft 1½in
Width over corner posts: 6ft 9in
Height to trolley plank: – 15ft 2in
Height inside lower saloon: – 6ft 6¾in
Stairs: – Direct 90°
Seats (lower saloon): – 24 LU
Seats upper saloon): – 29 TW 2+2
Trucks: – Peckham Cantilever; 6ft wheelbase; 31¾in diameter wheels
Motors: – 2 x GE 58; 30hp
Controllers: – BTH B18
Brakes: – Hand wheel electric and mechanical track

The classic 'Birkenhead' tramcars operated in Bristol for 40 years. No 220 is seen at Old Market on 6 April 1930 and No 7 at Horfield depot on 16 September 1937. Note the headlamp position, outside brake staff, wire mesh lifeguards and the advertisement panel fixed to the platform scrollwork behind the stairs. *Both H. B. Priestley*

Blackburn Corporation Tramways 1900 Milnes Standard bogie car. *E. Thornton*

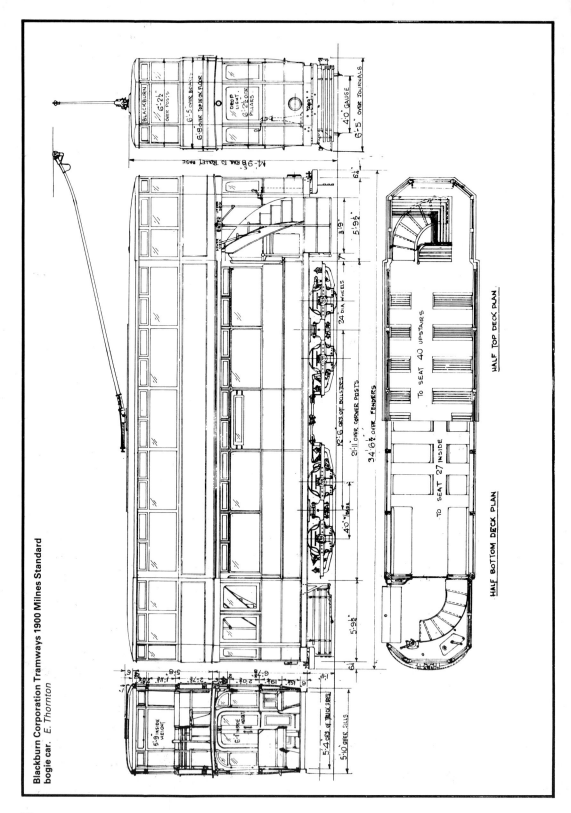

HALF TOP DECK PLAN

HALF BOTTOM DECK PLAN

To seat 40 upstairs

To seat 27 inside

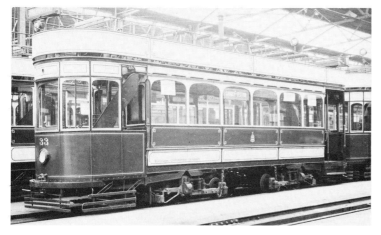

Blackburn No 33 when built at Birkenhead in 1899 was similar to the Middlesbrough cars. Seen in Intack depot the car was fitted with canopies and vestibules in 1906. *W. A. Camwell*

Blackburn Corporation Tramways Nos 36-75
Built: Hadley 1900
Length overall: – 35ft 8½in/34ft 6½in
Length over corner posts: – 23ft 0½in/21ft 11in
Length of platforms: – 5ft 10in/5ft 9½in
Width overall: – 6ft 6in
Width over corner posts: – 6ft 2½in
Height to trolley plank: – 15ft 4½in (when top-covered)
Height inside lower saloon: – 6ft 1in
Height inside upper saloon: – 5ft 9in
Stairs: – Direct 90°
Seats (lower saloon): – 32 LW (27 TU 2+1 when top-covered)
Seats (upper saloon): – 40 TW 2+1
Trucks: – Peckham Equal wheel bogies, Type 14B; 4ft wheelbase; 24in diameter wheels
Motors: – 4 x GE 526T; 20hp (some later re-motored)
Controllers: – BTH B6
Brakes: – Hand wheel, rheostatic
Gauge: – 4ft 0in

The cars were solidly built with five side windows and opening lights above, two to each window, which opened inwards at the top except for those at each end which pivoted. They had polished longitudinal seats in the lower saloon and transverse above.

Eight of these cars remained open-top until withdrawn; the rest received top covers built to match the lower saloons with square windows and opening lights. They also received more powerful motors and upholstered transverse seats in the lower saloon, and to allow operation under low railway bridges the original Peckham equal-wheel bogies were fitted with smaller diameter wheels thereby lowering the overall height of the car. This can be seen clearly in photographs and it could be argued that the lowest step was now redundant.

The Blackburn tramcars had very distinctive panelled dashes which gave them a solid angular appearance, accentuated by the unbroken glass screens of the vestibuled platforms. These retained their lattice gates, and the saloon was entered by double sliding doors. Inside, 'The regulations for working the services in fog' were displayed on the bulkheads, and the ceilings were of veneered wood. The upper saloons were spartan with polished wood dominant. Except for two cars, Nos 48 and 62, there were no bulkheads, and this gave them a spacious, open appearance. The best feature to my mind was the curved seat at each end; these faced outwards and gave one an excellent view forward. Destination equipment was minimal, consisting of a small blind at the top of each end and another in the centre window on each side of the lower saloon.

The Blackburn cars were dignified and stately with a reasonable turn of speed, especially on the Church section, which was open country beyond Intack depot. The cars were maintained in superb condition and their olive green livery, lined out in dark red and gold, set them off to perfection. They carried no advertisements and offered a smooth ride, even over the worn tracks in their final years.

The stately trams of Blackburn were built by Milnes in 1900 and lasted for almost 50 years. No 75 in its final form emerges from Intack depot. *W. A. Camwell*

Hurst Nelson

Hurst Nelson & Co Ltd was incorporated in 1899, and a large works was constructed alongside the Caledonian Railway's main line at Motherwell to build railway wagons of all types. The firm was taken over by Charles Roberts & Co Ltd of Wakefield in 1950 and the works closed in 1959. Although they formed only a small percentage of the total output, tramcars would appear to have been a profitable sideline as over 1,200 bodies and over 1,600 complete tramcars were constructed. In addition, underframes, top covers and thousands of minor items of tramcar equipment were supplied, mainly to the London County Council Tramways which purchased over 1,000 of the tramcars.

The first tram to be built, a sample car for Manchester Corporation Tramways, was delivered in 1899; with a Manchester-built top cover No 102 survived until 1929. The first large order was a sub-contract from the BTH company for 100 tramcars for London United Tramways. They were built to the London company's design with six 'Tudor Arch' windows and two-part stairs with a landing halfway. The bogies and electrical equipment were imported from the USA.

During 1900 Hurst Nelson set out to build complete tramcars, and the 10 open-top reversed-stair cars supplied to Ayr Corporation Tramways the following year are representative. The bodies were of the usual wooden frame construction with extended canopies, three windows of the 'Tudor Arch' type and ventilating lights above. Inside, the saloon was panelled with oak and sycamore, but the tapestry curtains did not last long.

The well-polished slatted, wooden longitudinal benches seated 22 passengers, the norm one might say for the 16ft body, and on top 'New London Dry-seats' took another 35. The cars were mounted on Hurst Nelson's patented cantilever trucks fitted with roller bearings. Unfortunately the bearings gave trouble and had to be replaced within a year.

Ayr Corporation Tramways Nos 1-10
Built: Motherwell 1901
Length overall: – 27ft 0in
Length over corner posts: – 16ft 0in
Width overall: – 6ft 10in
Stairs: Reversed 90°
Seats (lower saloon): – 22 LW polished wood
Seats (upper saloon): – 35 TW 2+2
Trucks: – HN patent cantilever; 6ft wheelbase; 30in diameter wheels
Motors: – 2 x BTH GE 52; 25hp
Controllers: – BTH B18
Brakes: – Hand wheel, rheostatic

Six similar cars (Nos 11-16), but with normal stairs and seating two more passengers, followed in 1902. Later cars supplied were Nos 19-20 in 1907, 21-22 in 1913 and 23-24 in 1915. These cars had flat-topped windows, Hurst Nelson 21E type trucks, and for the last two, open canopy top covers.

Hurst Nelson continued in its quest to supply a complete range of tramcars and in 1901 produced a maximum traction truck to its own design. This was fitted to the 12 bogie cars supplied to Blackpool in that year. These cars, Nos 42-53, four-window versions of those supplied to Ayr, were subsequently top-covered and enclosed, in stages, and No 49 is now preserved at the National Tramway Museum.

In 1905 12 open-top cars were supplied to the Mansfield & District Light Railways. These had three-window bodies, short canopies and direct stairs, which gave them an old-fashioned look, but seven of them survived in original condition until the system closed in October 1932. Although these cars were supplied with square-top windows, the company had a liking for the 'Tudor Arch' style and built them right up to 1925. Probably the last to be

Hurst Nelson built tramcars for a number of Scottish systems over the years. Ayr No 6 was typical of the open-top design with three saloon windows and reversed stairs. The detail shows longitudinal seating and roof construction.
Both Motherwell District Libraries Hurst Nelson collection

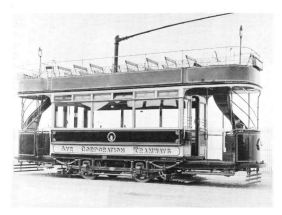

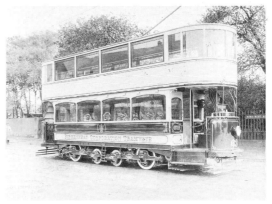

built in this style became Blackpool Nos 150-152.

The London County Council Tramways, with over 1,000 of its fleet built at Motherwell, was by far the most important Hurst Nelson customer, and from 1906 the company was manufacturing the very successful LCC Type 4 bogie on a large scale. As a result the truck could be supplied at a competitive price and was fitted to Birkenhead Nos 61-66, lowbridge double-deck cars, in 1916, and was later supplied to West Ham Corporation and the Dublin United Tramways Co.

The truck was a strengthened version of the Mountain & Gibson maximum traction swing bolster design. The bolster, the central transverse member on which the car body rides, was not a rigid part of the truck, but had a swinging-floating action, within fixed limits. This gave good riding qualities and a smoother movement round curves.

A further result of the link with the LCC Tramways was that the LCC design of car, or modifications of it, could be supplied to other customers. Thus Croydon Nos 31-55 were based on the 'E1' design, and Glasgow Nos 1091-1120, all enclosed four-window cars, were not dissimilar.

The last trams to be built at Motherwell were 11 modern metal framed cars for Edinburgh Corporation in 1934-35, numbered 231, 239, 240 and 11-18. They were built in one piece and had to be delivered by road to the Shrubhill works where final assembly took place. This was a distinct break from the traditional for Hurst Nelson, but the possibilities of this method of construction, if there were any, were not followed up and Edinburgh built all future cars at its Shrubhill works on Hurst Nelson underframes.

Nearly all Hurst Nelson tramcars were delivered by rail in two halves, lower saloon and top deck, as were the products of the other companies, but with the works close to the tracks of the Lanarkshire Traction Co, the trams for that company, the Paisley company and, possibly, Glasgow Corporation could be delivered under their own power.

Above left:
Ayr Nos 21-22 were built in 1913 with extended platforms and an additional exit under the stairs. They received Hurst Nelson top-covers in 1920 and were rebuilt in 1931 only to be scrapped at the end of the same year when the Ayr Corporation Tramways closed.
Motherwell District Libraries Hurst Nelson collection

Above:
Birkenhead No 63 was a lowbridge double-deck car built in 1916 and fitted with LCC type bogies.
Motherwell District Libraries Hurst Nelson collection

The Hurst Nelson designers did not progress far beyond the wooden-framed traditional tramcar; their trams were solidly built and almost as good as new when scrapped 30 or so years later. There was little evidence of drooping platforms, body movement and rattling windows as the Glasgow cars ran their last miles in 1960.

British Electric Car

The British Electric Car Co Ltd, was promoted in 1900, but delays in constructing the new works at Trafford Park, Manchester, resulted in the earliest orders, including that for Nottingham Nos 58-67 of 1901, being sub-contracted to G. F. Milnes.

To enter what was becoming a very competitive market and to undercut the established firms, the company designed a 'no frills' standard car. The main features were three side windows with straight tops and ventilators above, opening inwards at the top; extended canopies; and 180° reversed stairs. The latter was a new feature, later used at Preston, with two advantages – it was easier for the passengers to negotiate, and it gave drivers an improved view forward. Other features of the 'standard car' included fluted corner posts, canopy brackets made up of four circles within a circle, and upper deck railings of single scrolls. The saloon doors were outside-hung, single and offset from the centre.

There were variations to meet individual customers' needs, especially to the saloon doors and staircases. The 30 cars supplied to the Blackpool, St Annes & Lytham Tramways Co Ltd in 1903, for example, had a single central saloon door and 90° reversed stairs, while Paisley District Nos 1-40 had direct spiral stairs and twin leaf central doors. Huddersfield Corporation Tramways was the best customer with 44 cars supplied, mainly of the standard type as detailed in the next chapter.

The company built few bogie cars; apart from LCC Nos 376-401 of Class D and LUT Nos 212-236 of Type W built to drawings supplied, there were only the 20 cars for Salford Corporation (Nos 131-150) and the one car for the Trafford Park Estates Co tramway. These followed the style of the

Huddersfield Corporation Tramways Nos 33-42
Built: Trafford Park 1902
Length overall: – 27ft 6in
Length over corner posts: – 16ft 0in
Width overall: – 7ft 0in
Width over corner posts: – 6ft 9in
Height to trolley plank: – 9ft 9½in
Height inside lower saloon: – 6ft 9in
Height inside upper saloon: – 5ft 6in (when fitted Milnes-Voss top cover; not No 42)
Stairs: – Reversed 180°
Seats (lower saloon): – 22 LW
Seats (upper saloon): – 33 TW 2+2
Trucks: – BEC SB60; 6ft wheelbase
Motors: – 2 x Westinghouse 80; 35hp
Controllers: – Westinghouse 90M
Brakes: – Hand wheel, rheostatic, slipper
Gauge: – 4ft 7¾in

Blackpool, St Annes & Lytham Tramways Co Ltd Nos 1-30
Built: Trafford Park 1903
Length overall: – 27ft 6in
Length over corner posts: – 16ft 0in
Length of platforms: – 5ft 3in
Width overall: – 7ft 0in
Width over corner posts: – 6ft 9in
Height to trolley plank: – 9ft 9½in
Height inside lower saloon: – 6ft 9in
Stairs: – Reversed 90°
Seats (lower saloon): – 22 LW
Seats (upper saloon): – 32 TW 2+2
Trucks: – BEC SB60; 6ft wheelbase
Motors: – 2 x GE 52; 25hp
Controllers: – BTH

Milnes cars supplied to Nottingham but incorporated the fluted corner posts, 90° reversed stairs and the BEC canopy brackets.

The company also marketed its own truck, but this was of lightweight construction and unable to stand up to intensive urban use, although those supplied to Lytham lasted until tramway abandonment in 1937.

In spite of all its efforts the company failed to compete successfully for sales and a liquidator was appointed at the end of 1903. He failed to sell the business as a going concern and the works finally closed early in 1905. The last cars to be built were probably Bury Corporation Tramways Nos 29-34 which had been delivered the previous December. These were of the standard design with open balcony covers.

The works, together with the Milnes factory at Hadley, was purchased by the Electric Railway & Tramway Carriage Works Ltd in May 1905 when the United Electric Car Co Ltd was formed. The machinery was removed early in 1906 and the works remained empty until purchased by the Ford Motor Co to assemble, and later build, motor cars.

Over a four-year period only 478 tramcars were built at the Trafford Park works, approximately one-quarter of the planned output of 400 annually. The firm entered the market too late and the quality of its product was not up to the standard of the other companies: most of its tramcars had to be rebuilt within a few years.

The 'No frills' standard car

Below left:
No 6, with 90° reversed stairs, was built by British Electric Car Co in 1903 for the Blackpool, St Annes & Lytham Tramways Co Ltd on a BEC SB 60 truck. Taken over by Lytham St Annes Corporation, it was the only car to be fitted on to a Brill 21E. *Courtesy R. Brook*

Below:
The 40 cars supplied to the Paisley District Co featured 180° direct stairs, later standardised on Preston products. No 1 survived as Glasgow Corporation No 1001 until September 1935, latterly being used for conveying PW employees. *N. B. Traction collection*

3. Development of the Traditional Tram

As we have seen, there was little progress in tramcar design once the double-deck extended-canopy car, with or without top-cover, had become the standard product of the major builders. The product of 1925 was basically the same in appearance as that of 1910 except that the vestibules and balcony ends had been enclosed. The introduction of upholstered seating in the lower saloon and improved lighting had made the tram more comfortable, and improved motors had increased the speed, but it still tended to be draughty and cold in winter.

The majority of the smaller undertakings, municipal or otherwise, used the same trams, generally unaltered, from the day they opened to the day they closed. Examples include the Wrexham & District Electric Traction Co Ltd (a BET subsidiary) operating 12 Brush open-top reversed stair cars over 4½ miles of route from 1903 to 1927, and Ipswich Corporation with 36 similar cars over nearly 11 miles from 1903 to 1926.

The larger undertakings bought new trams in batches as the system expanded and traffic increased. After the initial purchase of 25 open-top vehicles from Brush in 1904, Derby Corporation Tramways bought in penny numbers. Eleven separate contracts, ranging from two to nine cars, were needed to bring the fleet up to its maximum of 78 by 1927. Derby trams operated for 30 years with many of the open-top cars fitted with balcony top-covers or rebuilt to the all-enclosed design.

The object of rebuilding was to improve passenger comfort and so attract new traffic as competition from motorbuses increased. The older trams were rebuilt, often in stages, and took many forms. This process is best illustrated by considering three of the municipal systems; Preston with a population of 117,000 in 1922, Nottingham with 262,000 and Huddersfield with 110,000.

Preston Corporation Tramways

This was the smallest of the three systems with a fleet of 48 cars and 10½ miles of route. Nos 1-26 were built in 1904 to the old uncanopied design with three curved-top windows, as were the four bogie versions, Nos 27-30. These latter remained unaltered until withdrawn but the single truck cars, except Nos 14-16, were fitted with top covers during 1907-13 and a number were vestibuled.

Nos 31-33 were single-deck bogie cars delivered in 1912 for the Ashton route, while Nos 34-39, delivered two years later, were some of the oddest looking cars to be built at the Dick Kerr works and gave the impression that the company was using up whatever materials were immediately to hand: nothing matched! The three windows of the lower saloon had curved tops with square ventilators above, while the four windows of the upper saloon were rectangular with curved top ventilators. The platforms were vestibuled while the balconies had the sides nearest the bulkhead glazed with curved top windows similar to those on the Manx Electric Railway saloon cars. Seating was longitudinal on both decks and two passengers could sit, facing outwards, on each balcony.

Preston Corporation Tramways opened on 7 June 1904 with open-top short roof cars built at the Dick Kerr works in Strand Road. No 6 is seen here in original conditions – direct stairs, curved top windows, glass ventilators and air scoops. *Courtesy F. K. Pearson*

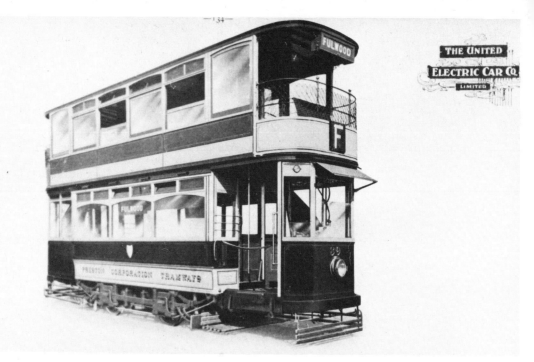

THE UNITED
ELECTRIC CAR CO.
LIMITED

Above:
Preston No 39 as built in 1914 with unmatched window arrangement and partially glazed balconies. Most municipal undertakings were anxious to provide maximum covered accommodation at this time. Note also the collapsible blind to help keep the rain off the driver's windscreen and the lift-up step to the platform. *GEC Traction*

Below:
Preston No 30 was one of the three lowbridge enclosed cars built at Deepdale Road for the Ashton route in 1926-27.
R. Elliott

However, the design was a considerable advance on the earlier uncanopied cars as it provided more seats and additional protection to both passengers and crew without the added weight and expense of an enclosed top deck. Incidentally, the top covers fitted to the earlier cars were of similar pattern but with five windows, the three inside ones having opening vents above. The smaller windows of the top covers could be opened individually without the need for the ratchet winding gear.

Preston Corporation Tramways No 30
Built: Deepdale Road 1926
Length overall: – 28ft 6in
Length over corner posts: – 16ft 0in
Length of platform: – 5ft 5in
Width overall: – 7ft 1in
Width over corner posts: – 6ft 9in
Height to trolley plank: – 15ft 0¼in
Height inside lower saloon: – 5ft 10½in
Height inside upper saloon: – 5ft 10½in
Stairs: – Direct 180°
Seats (lower saloon): – 22 LW
Seats (upper saloon): – 40 TW 2+2
Trucks: – Preston flexible axle; 7ft 0in wheelbase; 31¾in diameter wheels
Motors: – 2 x DK; 40hp
Controllers: – DK DB 1
Brakes: – Hand wheel, rheostatic

The Preston fleet was completed with second-hand purchases – nine single-deck cars from Sheffield in 1919 and three top-covered balcony cars from Lincoln in 1929.

Top covered cars could not pass under the low bridge carrying the LNWR main line over the Fylde Road on the Ashton route, and in 1926, following the rejection of a tender from the English Electric Co for a new lowbridge enclosed car, it was decided to build one in the tramway workshops. In the event three cars, Nos 30, 40 and 42, fitted with new motors and electrical equipment, emerged from the Deepdale Road workshops during 1926-27. Apparently built up from trams withdrawn at the time, they were traditional in appearance and true hybrids; they remain to the credit of the workshop staff who solved a rolling stock problem at minimum cost.

No 30 had a new, but more likely a re-posted, lower saloon with four side windows with lights above, but the four windows of the upper saloon were of the 'Tudor Arch' style. No 42 was similar, but the top deck of No 40 had square windows and lights to match those of the lower saloon. Each saloon had a headroom of 5ft 10½in, and the cars were fitted with new lightweight motors and 7ft wheelbase trucks.

Although a number of the other cars were enclosed and speeded up Preston did not continue to exploit these ideas and the trams finally ceased running in December 1935.

Nottingham Corporation Tramways

The city tramways totalled 25½ miles and a fleet of 200 cars had been built up by 1927. Bought from four different makers there was considerable variety of body style which became even more varied as rebuilding proceeded.

The original fleet of 105 open-top cars was delivered between 1900 and 1902. Nos 1-57 and 90-105 from Preston were of the 'Liverpool' type with three-window saloons, canopies, 90° reversed stairs and Brill 21E trucks. Nos 58-67, subcontracted from BEC were similar and built at Birkenhead, while Nos 78-83 from Hadley were also of the three-window design. All 16 bogie cars, Nos 68-77 and 84-89, were built at Hadley with the standard four-window body and reversed stairs; the first batch had 27G bogies and were later top-covered, but the last six, on 22E bogies, remained as built and were only used for football matches, etc. No 76 was fitted with an enclosed top-deck and was unique in Nottingham.

There was a gap of five years before the next series of cars were ordered, from Milnes Voss, Brush and the United Electric Car Co. These were all of the open-balcony type with three- four- or six-window bodies with normal stairs. The latter cars, Nos 126-135 from UEC in 1912, were of the semi-convertible type in that the lower saloon windows could be lowered halfway on fine days to emulate the open car.

The last new cars, of the open-balcony vestibuled type in 1920 and enclosed on both decks in 1927, came from the (by now) English Electric works at Preston. These had four-window bodies and P22 trucks, and were numbered 156-180 and 181-200 respectively.

In the meantime, there had been a massive rebuilding programme. Between 1904 and 1914 nearly all the open-top single-truck cars received new canopy top covers and normal stairs, but the extra weight of the covers had a detrimental effect on the pillars of the old lower saloons. To solve the problem new lower saloons were bought from Brush and UEC/EE, and with further covers supplied by Milnes Voss, in addition to the firms listed above, hardly any two cars were alike.

The newer cars with four air-scoops had larger than usual ventilating windows in the lower saloon, which, unusually, opened by lowering rather than sliding, pivoting in the centre or by being hinged at the bottom. The three windows of the upper saloon could be lowered by ratchet to about one-third of the window depth. A feature of the enclosed cars was the ceiling of the upper saloon in which the panelling was made up of alternate dark and light strips of polished wood.

The open balcony car in its many guises was dominant in the city from 1914 onwards, and although the last cars to be delivered were

enclosed on both decks, Nottingham was destined never to see a modern tram, unless the domed-roof Southampton cars, which followed the ring road en-route to Leeds in 1949, can be described as modern.

Nottingham contrasts

Above:
No 131 of the 'semi-convertible' type was built at Preston in
1912. Note the contrast between the elaborate six-window saloon and the plain three-window top cover. *R. Elliott*
Below:
No 139 of 1914 with a four-window saloon shows a similar construction style to No 131 with drop ventilating sashes. Both cars were photographed at Trent Bridge in 1931. *R. Elliott*
Right:
The final development was the arrival of 20 enclosed cars from Preston in 1927. No 192 is seen near the Market Place. *M. J. O'Connor*

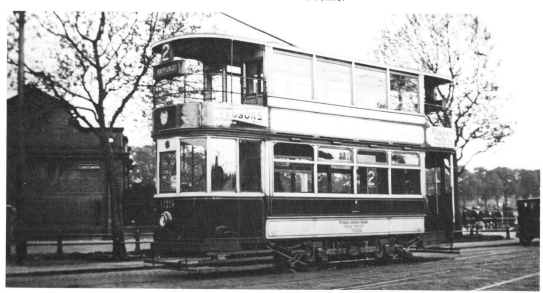

Huddersfield Corporation Tramways

Huddersfield was the first municipality to own and operate its own tramway system. Starting with steam traction from Fartown to Lockwood on 11 January 1883, the system expanded and, electrified, reached a total of 38 route miles with 11½ miles beyond the municipal boundaries.

Huddersfield purchased its electric tramcars from only three sources; 25 open-top bogie cars came from G. F. Milnes, 45 open-top single truck cars from BEC and 74 top-covered cars from the UEC/EE works at Preston.

The Milnes cars, Nos 1-25, among the first to be built at the new Hadley works, were to the older short-roof design with five-window bodies and seats for 56 passengers (24 inside, 32 out). The 22E bogies were later replaced by Brill or Mountain & Gibson 21E trucks.

The BEC cars were delivered between 1901 and 1903. First came Nos 26-31 with three side windows of the 'Tudor Arch' type with hinged lights above them. The bulkhead windows on each side of the sliding saloon doors were also of this style. Four of the cars were of the short roof design with direct 90° stairs, but Nos 27 and 31 had extended canopies and the new BEC 180° reversed stair. The saloon entrance on these cars had to be offset to allow for the new staircase.

Following No 32, a three-window 'one-off' reversed stair car, came Nos 33-42 of the BEC design described earlier, but the next batch (Nos 43-56, 40 and 63-66) were of the short-roof type with normal stairs. (No 40 should have been numbered 62. It replaced a car damaged in an accident which was later rebuilt and re-numbered 62). Nos 57-61 and 68-70 were all of the standard design, with No 59 having a superior interior finish for the 1902 Tramways Exhibition. No 67 was an American-built car with four rounded-top side windows which was bought at a bargain price in 1903. All the BEC cars were fitted with the SB60 truck, but within 10 years these had all been replaced by 21E and 21EM types.

A number of the above cars were delivered fitted with Milnes Voss 'Magrini' top-covers, including No 40 and Nos 63-66. The covers proved unsuitable and the Department was soon experimenting with 'Do it Yourself' types based on the 'Bailey' cover used at nearly Bradford.

These new covers did not extend beyond the saloon bulkheads and had three or four opening windows. The first three-window covers were fitted to some of the BEC reversed-stair cars and the four-window version to five-window Milnes cars. A shorter three-window cover, 12ft instead of 16ft, was fitted to a few more of the BEC cars. Further variations had three or four windows, some with fixed coloured quarter lights.

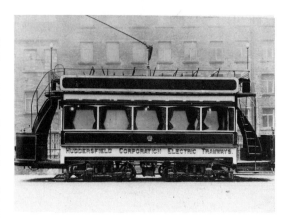

Above:
The Huddersfield Milnes bogies of 1900 were among the first cars to be built at the new Hadley works. As originally built with short roof and direct stairs on Brill 22E maximum traction bogies. These were found to be unsuitable and were replaced by single trucks of the 21E type. All were eventually top covered and No 9 with a four drop window cover is seen at Sheepridge. *Both courtesy R. Brook*

In 1912 a new six-window cover with ventilating lights was designed and fitted to five BEC cars. These covers were built by UEC, and further covers to this design were fitted to the remaining open-top Milnes car. Finally two BEC cars (Nos 42 and 68) were rebuilt circa 1924, and the 11 Milnes and 13 BEC cars which had been fitted with the home-made covers were rebuilt during 1927-33 with extended canopies and platform vestibules.

Huddersfield was a progressive tramway undertaking and from 1909 onwards purchased its tramcars from the car works at Preston. Each batch

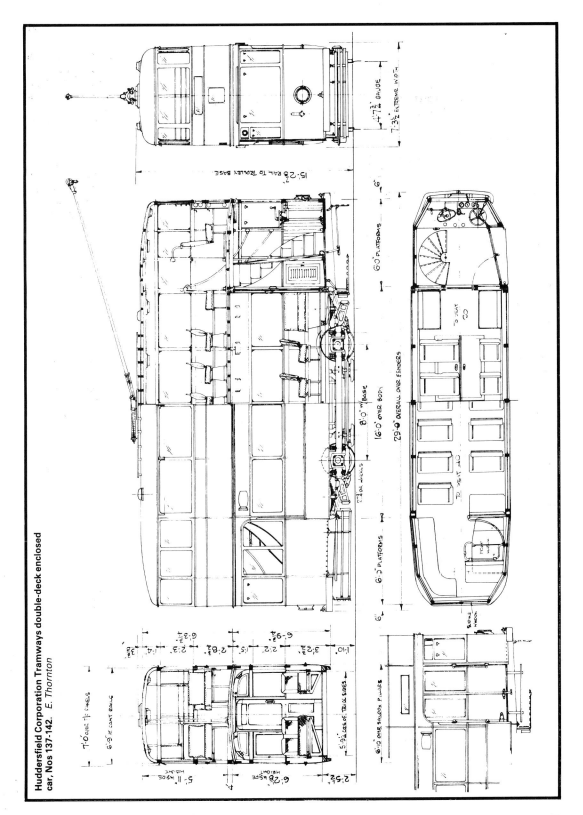

Huddersfield Corporation Tramways double-deck enclosed car, Nos 137-142. *E. Thornton*

of cars was an improvement on the previous ones, as follows:

Cars	Date	Remarks
71-75	1909	Open platforms, later vestibuled; open-canopy top decks
76	1910	Open platform, later vestibuled; front exit and enclosed top deck. (Built at Preston, but modified as above before entering service).
77-86	1912	Vestibuled platforms with doors; open-canopy top decks.
87-96	1913	Vestibuled platforms with doors; open canopy top decks.
97-106	1914	As above, but with bodies 6in wider over sills and almost straight rocker panels.
107-126	1919/20	Vestibuled platforms; open-canopy top decks.
127-136	1923	Vestibuled platforms; enclosed top decks but with the narrower sill width and concave rocker panels.

All the above cars had four-window 16ft bodies and, with the exception of No 76, direct 180° spiral stairs. All had Preston built trucks; 21Es on Nos 71-96, Peckham P22s on Nos 97-106, and the 21E wide-wing type on Nos 107-136.

The distinguishing features on all these cars were the quarter lights on both decks and no air scoops. All the lights were hinged at the bottom except for the end two on the top deck which were fixed. The upper deck windows could also be opened. The 6ft platforms gave the cars wider front screens and a flat ended appearance, while the entrance to the upper saloon on Nos 71-126 (except 76) was offset to the left of the centre line to give a larger circulating area immediately inside the upper saloon. On the canopy was a seat for five plus the seat for two, facing forward, which was always there on Nos 77-126, and on Nos 71-75 after delivery of Nos 77-86 in 1912. A new feature was to fit the Board of Trade light on a box at the top of the vestibule near the entrance. On Nos 71 onwards this position also displayed the fleet number.

At Huddersfield we have traced the development of the traditional tramcar and its final form was to be seen in Nos 137-144, delivered from the Preston works in 1931 with the last two in 1932. The domed roof 'smoothed off' four-window body had a wooden frame, but 'Ashanco' air extractors had replaced the traditional ventilators. Technically the cars were advanced, being fitted with Maley & Taunton swing link trucks of 8ft wheelbase and with Hoffman roller bearings. There were six methods of applying the brakes, an asset in a town as hilly as Huddersfield.

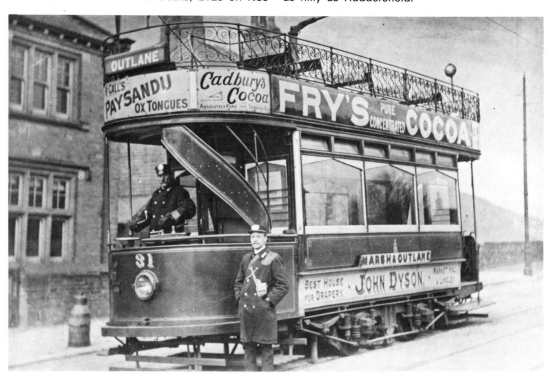

Left and above:
Two of the six BEC cars supplied to Huddersfield in 1901-02, Nos 27 and 31, had extended canopies, 'Tudor Arch' windows and the new 180° reversed staircase. No 31 is shown as built at Outlane terminus: it later received a three-window top cover. BEC standard car No 68, as fitted with a three-window top-cover, was photographed at Sheepridge terminus. *Both courtesy R. Brook*

Huddersfield Corporation Tramways Nos 137-142
Built: Preston 1931
Length overall: – 29ft 0in
Length over corner posts: – 16ft 0in
Length of platforms: – 6ft 0in
Width overall: – 7ft 0in
Width over corner posts: – 6ft 10in
Height to trolley plank: – 15ft 2⅞in
Height inside lower saloon: – 6ft 2⅛in
Height inside upper saloon: – 5ft 11in
Stairs: – Direct 180°
Seats (lower saloon): – 20 TU 2+1 moquette
Seats (upper saloon): – 38 TU 2+2 dark red leather
Trucks: – M&T Swing link; 8ft wheelbase; 27¾in diameter wheels
Motors: – 2 x EE 105-5H; 50hp
Controllers: – DB1 Form K33E
Brakes: – Hand wheel, rheostatic, air wheel and track, magnetic track
Gauge: – 4ft 7¾in

The main advance in Nos 137-144 was in passenger comfort. Gone were the wooden ceilings and the rows of light bulbs protruding along each side, the dark wooden longitudinal seating in the lower saloon and the upper saloon bulkhead doors. The saloons were now light and airy with the ceilings of aluminium stippled white and panelled with mahogany strips. Lighting in both saloons was recessed into the concave sides of the ceilings, the shades having chromium-plated rims. All handrails and stair rails were finished in 'Staybrite', and the three rails following the contours of the upper saloon ends, above seat level, were a marked feature. Furthermore, controller tops, brake handles and wheels were also chromium plated.

The seating was attractive with the transverse seats of the lower saloon trimmed in moquette with leather facings and those of the upper saloon in dark red leather. Total seating capacity was 58 except for the last two cars which were 1ft longer and seated four more in the upper saloon.

The cars were sold to Sunderland Corporation Tramways in 1938 and entered service there with the minimum of alteration because red and cream was the common livery. The route number space was blocked in, the platform doors removed and

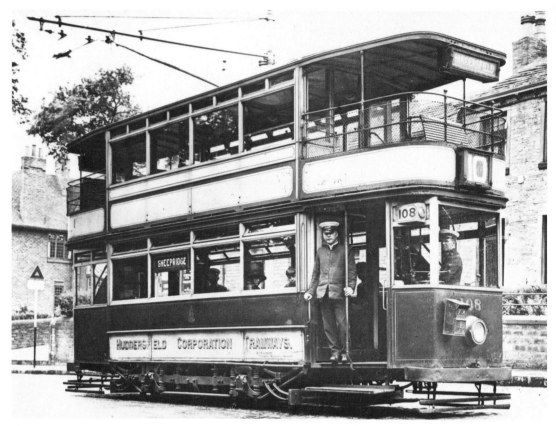

Above:

The main feature of the Huddersfield 'Preston' cars was the width of the front vestibule window which is shown clearly in this view of No 108 at Sheepridge terminus. Note the fleet number on the Board of Trade light box. *Courtesy R. Brook*

Below:

Hailed by the transport press of the time as 'unsurpassed in the provinces', Huddersfield Nos 137-144 with domed roof and platform doors were neat, practical cars. This is No 141 at Longroyd Bridge depot. *M. J. O'Connor*

pantographs fitted in place of the trolley poles. The trucks were altered from the Huddersfield gauge of 4ft 7¾in to Sunderland's standard 4ft 8½in, and the new owner's name appeared on their sides. Numbered 29 to 36 in Sunderland they operated for a further 16 years.

In Sunderland they were far superior to the ex-Ilford Corporation cars built by Brush in 1932 to the traditional design, and they also compared well with those built for Sunderland at the same time – Nos 87-95 by English Electric and Nos 86 and 96-98 at the tramway workshops in Hylton Road. These cars were teak framed with aluminium panelling and cork insulation. Also straight sided, they were on EMB Hornless roller bearing trucks. The lower saloons were similar to the Huddersfield cars with a white ceiling and concealed lights, but the upper saloon still retained the top light ventilators with red and blue glass and also the light bulbs along each side of the flat white roof. The seating, 26+36, blue moquette in the lower saloon and red leather on top, was well up to the Huddersfield standard.

There is no doubt that the Huddersfield cars, with a simple straightforward body design, an attractive appearance and a good turn of speed, were superior to the contemporary bus or trolleybus, and these cars served both systems well.

4. The Modern Tramcar

The advent of the modern Huddersfield tramcars could be said to signify the re-awakening of the British tramcar industry after years of stagnation. At long last there were signs of inventiveness and innovation, and although this did not approach the great surge of interest shown at the beginning of the century, considerable progress was made. This was spurred on no doubt by the need for a vehicle that could offer a high carrying capacity with at least the same comfort and performance as the competing bus and trolleybus.

The traditional tramcar, constructed of high quality timber, and square and angular in appearance, had changed little in the previous 30 years. However, timber was becoming increasingly expensive and progress in bus design had seen the development of composite and all-steel bodies.

The modern tram body, following the lead given by the bus industry, was also built as a complete unit, and with the increasing use of metal the angular look gave way to a more rounded appearance, especially in the upper deck and roof. The increased strength of the new body construction also enabled the bulkheads to be

Modern or traditional?

In 1952 Sunderland Corporation operated a wide variety of tramcars of which 30 were purchased from other undertakings. All the cars illustrated were built within two years and show the changing styles. Portsmouth No 1 was built in 1930 and later became Sunderland No 45 as which it is seen at Fulwell. Seating 23 TU/30 TU, it was fitted with an EMB truck in 1938. *R. Brook*

dispensed with and so enhance the appearance of the interior.

The impetus for development came from the operators rather than the manufacturers, though as we shall see, the LCC Tramways was co-operating with the English Electric Co to produce a modern high capacity tramcar. In this chapter we will look at the impetus that came from the managers and engineers of the smaller systems as already illustrated by the Huddersfield cars built to the design and specification of the manager, Mr A. A. Blackburn. These cars came to Sunderland in 1938 because the manager there, Mr C. A. Hopkins, was in the process of modernising the tram fleet by the judicious purchase of secondhand cars. Among these was Portsmouth No 1 built in 1930 to the design of the manager, Mr Ben Hall. Purchased in

1936 and numbered 52 (later 45) in the Sunderland fleet, the four-widow body can be said to be traditional in design; but with a domed roof, smaller upper saloon windows and flattened rocker panels it had a modern appearance. The destination indicators blocked in the top windows at each end of the car and distracted from this, but they were removed at Sunderland and replaced by an opening window. The upper saloon windows were of the sliding type, doubtless advantageous in the warm summer air of the south coast town, but

Ex-Ilford car Sunderland No 4, built in 1932, has been vestibuled, and waits at the final Durham Road terminus. *R. Brook*

Above left:
Sunderland's own cars of this era were based on No 86 built at Hylton Road in 1932. No 89, on Dykelands Road, was one of nine cars built at Preston the following year.

Above:
Nos 26-28 of 1935 were probably the best of the new cars to run in Sunderland. Their simple, straightforward design and good looks are displayed by No 27 at Fulwell.

in Sunderland metal bars were fitted across them, presumably to prevent abuse.

Other second-hand purchases included traditional cars from Accrington (Sunderland Nos 19-20) in 1931, Ilford (Sunderland Nos 2-9) in 1937, Manchester (Sunderland Nos 37-42) in 1947, Bury (Sunderland No 85) in 1948, and two modern cars – the experimental Feltham (Sunderland No 100) in 1937, and a centre entrance car from South Shields (Sunderland No 48) in 1946.

In addition to these purchases 11 new tramcars entered service during the six years up to 1940. The first to arrive was No 99, a large centre-entrance bogie car built by English Electric in 1934 and similar in appearance to those being built for Blackpool at that time. In the following year came three round-dash cars with twin headlights numbered 26-28 and built in the Hylton Road workshops. The body frames of teak and ash were built on to steel underframes, and the four corner pillars were carried right up to the top-deck cant rails. The almost flat rocker panels were of ¾in steel plate and acted as trusses, so that even in their last days, 15 years later, the bodies were still sound.

The five-window lower saloons retained the traditional ventilating top lights except at each end where Ashanto air extractors were fitted, and in the centre where the destination screens were located. In addition each offside bulkhead had a half drop ventilating window. Although the main saloon windows were smaller than on the older cars the ventilating lights made the interior light and airy.

The upper saloon had fixed windows, except for one at each end and another above each staircase. With curved glass roof lights, six on each side, it was almost like riding on an open-top car, because there was so much light, even on a dull day!

The seating, for 64 passengers (23/36) was transverse; in the upper saloon there were two single seats in the centre to assist passenger flow or, more probably, to give the conductor more elbow room, and a single seat at each end facing forward. This gave the enthusiast and passenger a fine view, especially when crossing the Monkwearmouth Bridge or approaching the Gas Office junction.

The brown moquette seating harmonised with the aluminium side panels and ceilings which were lined with rexine, gold in the lower saloon and on the roof, with red on the upper saloon sides. The luxury appearance of the interior was completed with concealed lighting, and rubber tiling on the floors which also matched the colour scheme.

These were the best trams in the town and rode well on their modern EMB Hornless trucks of 9ft wheelbase and, like the Huddersfields, were simple in design, but they had an extra indefinable quality which lifted them out of the ordinary.

Mr Hopkins, however, favoured the centre entrance for public service vehicles and the remaining new cars were of this type. There were

---

Sunderland Corporation Tramways Nos 26-28
Built: Sunderland 1935
Stairs: – Direct 90°
Seats (lower saloon): – 28 TU 2+2 moquette
Seats (upper saloon): – 36 TU 2+2 moquette
Trucks: – EMB Hornless; 9ft wheelbase
Motors: – 2 x CP 161; 62hp
Controllers: – Allen West
Brakes: – Hand wheel, EMB air

---

two designs and the key feature was the specially adapted Maley & Taunton 9ft long wheelbase truck which incorporated a well section to take the centre entrance.

The Brush car, No 55 delivered in 1935, was similar to Nos 26-28 except for the centre entrance with platform doors, and air extractors instead of the traditional opening lights in the lower saloon. The seating and interior decor were also similar with blue moquette seating, rexine panelling and concealed lighting. The centre entrance and the straight staircases within each saloon reduced the capacity of the car by two double seats giving 24/36, and to me the lower saloons always seemed more cramped and darker than those of the previous three cars. No 54 was completed at Hylton Road in 1936 on a body frame supplied by Brush.

The English Electric Co supplied the body frames for cars Nos 49-53 which were completed at Hylton Road between April 1936 and May 1940. These cars had all the features of what may be termed the 'modern Preston look', with pointed fronts, double windscreens, twin headlights and destination indicators. The interior and seating arrangements were the same as on the Brush cars except that the straight stairs went direct from the platforms, but this did not allow an increase in seating capacity. The stairs were in the normal position; that is to the right of the entrance except for No 53 which had them on the left.

When I first visited Sunderland in July 1945 all the new, and most of the second-hand, cars were in

Sunderland Corporation Tramways No 53
Built: Sunderland 1936*
Length overall: – 32ft 0in
Width overall: – 7ft 0½in
Stairs: – Straight; left side of entrance
Seats (lower saloon): – 24 TU 2+2 moquette
Seats (upper saloon): – 36 TU 2+2 moquette
Trucks: – EE Cranked FL 32; 9ft wheelbase
Motors: – 2 x GEC WT28; 50hp
Controllers: – EE Z4
Brakes: – Hand wheel, Westinghouse air

* Underframe and bodyshell was supplied by English Electric, Preston

Sunderland Corporation Tramways No 55
Built: Loughborough 1935
Length overall: – 32ft 0in
Width overall: – 7ft 0½in
Stairs: – Straight; right side of entrance
Seats (lower saloon): – 24 TU 2+2 moquette
Seats (upper saloon): – 36 TU 2+2 moquette
Trucks: – M&T; 9ft wheelbase; cranked to clear centre entrance
Motors: – 2 x CP 161; 62hp
Controllers: – EE Z4

service, and as all the routes were short and an all-day ticket was available, it was possible to ride on all types of car in a few hours (except for the two

Photographed in Chester Road, No 51 displays the modern 'Preston' look. Although of English Electric design it was completed at Hylton Road in 1938.

bogie cars which always seemed to be at the back of Wheatsheaf depot).

During subsequent visits I spent a lot of time on the modern and ex-Huddersfield cars. These offered quick acceleration – an essential aspect on a system with four rush hours – and a high level of comfort. It could be argued that these cars were too comfortable for a system of short headways and frequent stops.

The policy of new cars and bargain buys in the second-hand market enabled Sunderland trams to survive until 1 October 1954 when nine cars, including four from Huddersfield, made a final run from Seaburn to the Wheatsheaf depot.

Moving north into Scotland, Dundee City Tramways operated 56 traditional tramcars over 12.24 miles of route. Supplied by all the major builders, the older cars, including nine 'own make' cars (Nos 29-33 and 53-56), had been rebuilt, but the pride of the fleet were Nos 19-28, the Lochee cars built by Brush in 1930. They were wider than the standard Dundee car and were used on the Lochee route which was double track and climbed continuously for two miles. These cars, among the last traditional cars to be built, had leather upholstered seating, and, with two 50hp motors, airbrakes and modern EMB 8ft 6in wheelbase trucks, could speed up the hill to Lochee terminus. The Dundee tramways closed on 21 October 1956.

In Aberdeen, 70 miles to the north, over 100 tramcars operated over approximately the same mileage as at Dundee. Here, however, the Corporation Tramways had to cater for hundreds of visitors during the holiday season and for this purpose had purchased second-hand cars from Nottingham in 1936 and Manchester in 1947.

Aberdeen had an interesting variety of tramcars and was a welcome change after the very standardised fleets of the other Scottish cities. It was a very efficiently run system, in many ways similar to Sunderland, with traditional, second-hand and modern tramcars. The older open-balcony cars still running in 1952 were mainly used as summer extras to the beach, as were the second-hand cars from Nottingham and Manchester, but the former had been scrapped by this time.

The modern cars dated from 1940 when two bogie (Nos 138 and 139), and two single truck cars (Nos 140 and 141) were purchased from English Electric. No more single truck cars were bought, but in 1949 a further 20 bogie cars were ordered from English Electric. These were built under sub-contract by R. Y. Pickering of Wishaw because Preston had ceased to build tramcars by this time. They were to the design of the prototypes with detailed improvements resulting from experience in traffic.

The underframe, including a well for the centre entrance, was of welded rolled steel sections and extremely rigid. The body was of oak reinforced with steel angles round the entrances and for strength and rigidity where necessary. The external body panelling was steel plate and the window mullions clad with aluminium sheeting. The livery was green and cream with the fleet numbers in chrome-plated numerals on each dash.

The entrance platform was only 1ft 4in from rail level and 4ft 6in wide. It was covered with studded rubber matting, and a further step took one into the lower saloon. Straight staircases, one on each side, led from the platform to the upper saloon, with the last two steps turning to give direct access to the upper saloon gangway. Quick acting jack-knife doors were fitted on either side of the platforms.

The driver had a separate cabin at each end stepped down from the lower saloon floor level. It could be entered from the street or through a bulkhead door from the saloon. The driver had a portable stool, and the cars were equipped with loudspeakers so enabling the driver to announce the stops as in modern continental practice.

The electrical equipment was by English Electric. The four motors were of 38hp each, and there was an impressive array of braking systems including the Maley & Taunton hand brake and EMB pattern air wheel brake.

Green was the dominant colour of the interior with different shades used to pick out the pattern on the green coloured background material on the ceiling and interior panels. The transverse

reversible seats supplied by G. D. Peters were of Dunlopillo and upholstered in green hide. In 1952 the seating was converted to longitudinal to improve passenger flow in the lower saloon and to ease the work of the conductor. Lights were concealed in fittings running the whole length of each saloon and tubular heaters were also provided, eight in the upper saloon and four in the lower. The light and airy nature of the upper saloon was further enhanced by glass eaves in the curves of the roof panels along each side.

When these cars were delivered in 1949 the Aberdeen tramways seemed sound for at least a further 20 years, but I well remember the works superintendent at that time sounding a warning: the new cars were expensive to operate because of their more complicated electrical equipment and he was pessimistic for the future. They were also expensive on labour and required two conductors, one for the lower saloon who also operated the single folding doors manually, and one for the upper. To overcome this, mechanically-operated folding double doors were fitted and worked

Eighteen of Nottingham's newest tramcars ended their days in Aberdeen. They retained their destination boxes at each end, and No 2 is seen at the Bridge of Don terminus. *R. Brook*

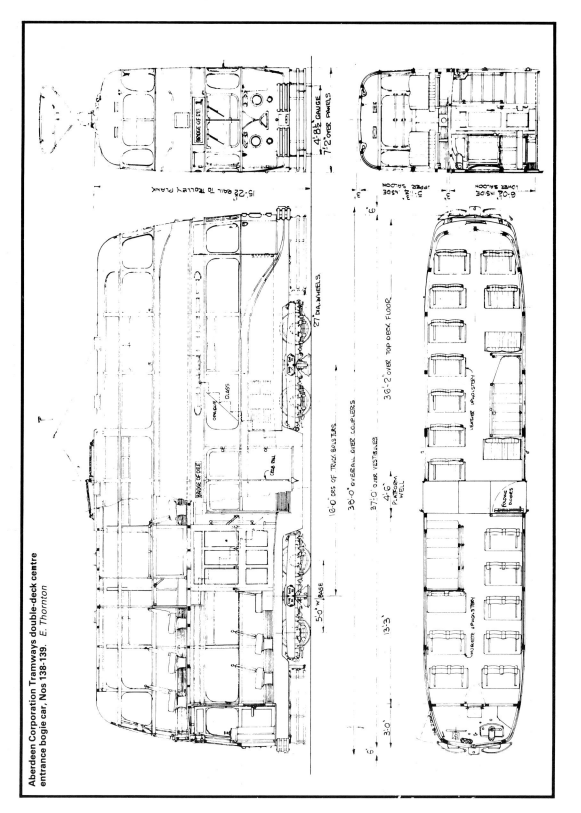

Aberdeen Corporation Tramways double-deck centre entrance bogie car, Nos 138-139. *E. Thornton*

4'8½ GAUGE
7'2" OVER PANELS

15'2½" RAIL TO TROLLEY PLANK

3'3" INSIDE UPPER SALOON

6'0½" INSIDE LOWER SALOON

27' DIA. WHEELS

16'0" CRS OF TRUCK BOLSTERS

38'0" OVERALL OVER COUPLERS

37'0" OVER VESTIBULES

4'6" PLATFORM WELL

36'2" OVER TOP DECK FLOOR

LEATHER UPHOLSTERY

MOQUETTE UPHOLSTERY

FOLDING DOORS

BRIDGE OF DEE

OPALINE GLASS

GRAB RAIL

5'0" W BASE

13'3"

3'0"

Aberdeen's dark green and white livery set off the 'Pilcher' tram to perfection. This is No 52 (ex-Manchester No 502) outside King Street works in April 1958.

Aberdeen Corporation Tramways Nos 19-38
Built: R. & Y. Pickering, Wishaw
Length overall: – 38ft 0ins
Length of platform: – 4ft 6in
Width overall: – 7ft 1¾in
Height to trolley plank: – 15ft 2½in
Height inside lower saloon: – 6ft 0¼in
Height inside upper saloon: – 5ft 11¾in
Stairs: – Straight
Seats (lower saloon): – 32 TU; 2+2 later 30 LU
Seats (upper saloon): – 44 TU 2+2
Trucks: – EMB lightweight; 5ft wheelbase; 27in diameter wheels
Motors: – 4 x EE 327; 38hp
Controllers: – EE Z type DB 1
Brakes: – Hand wheel, air-wheel, rheostatic and magnetic emergency

remotely by the motorman. The fitments included an illuminated caution sign and an emergency valve by the doorway. The permitted number of standing passengers was reduced from 20 to five (presumably to prevent interference with the door mechanism or for staff reasons), so reducing the overload capacity from 96 to 79 and hence their revenue-earning potential.

These fine cars provided the basic service on the trunk Bridges route, Bridge of Don – Bridge of Dee, and with feeder bus services from each terminus

the cars were well loaded throughout the day, or at least in summer when I visited Aberdeen. Latterly the cars were also used on the Hazlehead route.

The riding quality of these cars was superb and the rapid acceleration hardly noticeable; they were quiet running and comfortable. Their only shortcoming, in my opinion, was the restricted width of the front upper saloon seats and lack of leg room which resulted from the tapering nature of the bodywork.

The Aberdeen system closed on 3 May 1958 with a procession of six tramcars from the Bridge of Dee to King Street with the horse tram heading the procession from Holborn Junction, and No 36 with

Brush built two series of cars for Aberdeen: Nos 106-115 in 1925 and 126-137 in 1929. Similar to Dundee's Lochee cars, No 109 on a Brill 21E truck is outside Woodside depot on 4 August 1953.

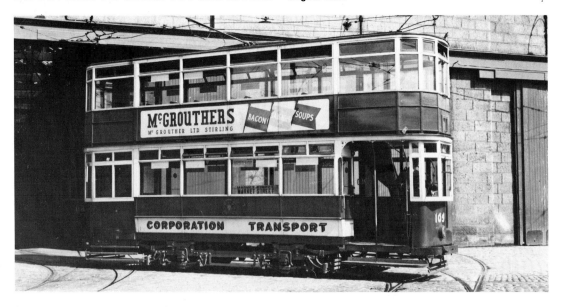

Modern trams in Aberdeen

Above:

Two bogie cars, Nos 138 and 139, and two single-truck cars, Nos 140 and 141, were built by English Electric in 1940. A further 20 cars were built by R. Y. Pickering in 1949, and No 33 of this series moves away down an almost deserted Albyn Place.

Left:

Traditional in appearance but fitted with modern equipment and upholstered seats were the Belfast 'Chamberlain' cars of 1930. In the new blue and cream livery they were the start of a new era. Brush-built No 353 was photographed in Crumlin Road on 6 June 1953.

official guests being the last car to turn into King Street depot. Thus Aberdeen lost its tramways. Here ran not only the most luxurious double-deck tramcars ever built, but also the last traditional open balcony cars with their faded photographs of local places of interest in the upper sections of the bulkheads, and their polished brass controller tops and brake handles.

Belfast, the centre of the only extensive urban area in Northern Ireland, had a well maintained tramway system which reached its climax in 1937 when 350 cars were operating over 51.47 route miles. All cars were single truck, the majority being

the three-window traditional 'Standard Red' described earlier, together with some horse cars rebuilt prior to 1910. New stock included 50 enclosed cars purchased from Brush in 1919. Numbered 292-341, they had been renovated, re-equipped electrically and fitted with new Maley & Taunton 8ft wheelbase swing-link trucks. They were followed in 1930 by another 50 cars, Nos 342-381 from Brush and Nos 382-391, built, or more probably assembled, at the Service Motor Works in Belfast. These cars, of traditional four side window design with ventilating lights, also had Maley & Taunton 8ft trucks, upholstered seats and modern equipment.

Finally, 50 modern streamlined trams, Nos 292-441, were purchased in 1935-36 to replace the older cars. These were built to the specification of the manager, Major (later Lt Col) R. McCreary, but the design work was carried out by the English Electric Co at Preston which built the first, No 392, and 19 others, Nos 423-441. The remainder were built or assembled at the Service Motor Works on frames from Hurst Nelson.

Belfast Corporation Tramways No 392
Built: Preston 1935
Length overall: – 32ft 0in
Stairs: – Direct 90°
Seats (lower saloon): – 24 TU 2+2
Seats (upper saloon): – 40 TU 2+2
Trucks: – Maley & Taunton swing-link; 8ft wheelbase
Motors: – 2 x Crompton Parkinson; 50hp
Controllers: – MV OK 27B (OK 34B on others of class)
Brakes: – Hand wheel, rheostatic, air and magnetic

Belfast's modern tramcars are represented by No 406. Built locally on a Hurst Nelson underframe it has a Maley & Taunton 8ft wheelbase truck and is seen in Scarbo Street, close by the County Down station.

These cars incorporated all the improvements in tramcar design noted earlier: entrance doors, air extractors, concealed lighting and transverse upholstered seating. The lower saloons of these cars with blue transverse leather seats for 24 passengers and white roof panelling were particularly spacious. The upper saloons were similar, but had double transverse seats for 40, also in blue leather, and opening end windows.

The cars were finished in an attractive blue livery, and the elaborate destination displays were more akin to those seen on contemporary buses and trolleybuses. All had airbrakes, and two, Nos 392-393, separate driver's compartments. Dropped platforms were a problem with the earlier cars and those built later were strengthened to overcome it. These cars were comfortable and fast, and in some ways reminiscent of Edinburgh, although they also had design links with the new cars for Liverpool. An attractive feature of all the Belfast cars was the clock on one of the lower saloon bulkheads; the only other cars known to have had these were some in Halifax.

Darwen Corporation operated one of England's smallest tramway systems with a maximum of 22 cars working 4.36 miles of route, and no doubt survived thanks to the joint service to Blackburn along the main road linking the two towns. This route was inaugurated by the Blackburn & Over Darwen Tramways Co with steam traction on 14 April 1882. Darwen's claim to fame was the purchase of two modern tramcars from English Electric in 1936. Narrow gauge versions of those being built for Blackpool, they must have caused quite a sensation when they entered service in the town. Numbered 23 and 24 they were of centre entrance design with maximum traction bogies and 2+1 transverse upholstered seating for 56 passengers. Other features included separate drivers compartments, twin headlamps and airbrakes.

When I first visited the town in December 1944 both cars were in the depot and it was not until July 1945 that I rode on No 23 from Blackburn to Darwen. By this time the car was noisy but still offered a comfortable ride. The two cars never realised their full potential, for following the closure of the Darwen tramways on 5 October 1946, they were purchased by the Llandudno & Colwyn Bay Electric Railway for service between the two resorts. Converted from 4ft to 3ft 6in gauge, they were restricted to local service only and spent most of their time in the depot at Church Road, Rhos-on-Sea, until that system closed on 31 March 1956.

5. Single-Deck Tramcars

By the time tramways were being electrified and extended the double-deck car had become the standard in Great Britain and, in contrast to the rest of Europe, the single-deck car remained the exception. Most tramway systems were in urban areas where the double-decker's higher carrying capacity could be used to advantage.

The Roundhay Park line in Leeds, the first in the country to use the overhead trolley system, and the Dearne District Light Railways, the last complete new system to be opened, both used single-deck cars. The former had six small single-deck cars and the latter 30 traditional five-window vestibuled cars from English Electric. Built in 1924 and mounted on P22 8ft 6in wheelbase trucks, they had very short platforms with entrances on each side – an interesting feature incorporated to permit one-man operation, but throughout the short nine-year life of the system conductresses were employed. The cars had longitudinal seating for 36 passengers, but four cars had 2+1 cushioned transverse seats fitted about 1927, which reduced their seating capacity to 31. On closure these four cars, plus one other, went

to Falkirk, where, shortened and reconstructed, they ran until 31 July 1937. A further four went to Lytham St Annes to become Nos 51-54 in the Corporation fleet.

The Dearne District had single-deck cars because the low bridge at Wath LMS station had a clearance of only 12ft 6in to the crown of the arch. The cars had two 40hp DK 30B motors but the average speed was only about 7mph as they were never able to show their paces on the single line system, and with long waits at the passing loops, easily succumbed to the competition waged by the Yorkshire Traction Co, successor to the Barnsley & District Electric Traction Co Ltd.

By far the largest exclusive user of single-deck vehicles was the Potteries Electric Traction Co Ltd, a BET company, because low bridges at Longton, Stoke and Fenton ruled out the use of double-deckers. On larger systems a low bridge would dictate the use of single-deck cars on one or more routes, as on the 53 route in Manchester. The problem was often solved by lowering the roadway under the offending bridge as at Brightside in

The Roundhay Park Tramway opened on 11 November 1891 with tramcars which were typical of early designs with six small windows and a clerestory roof.
R. Brook collection

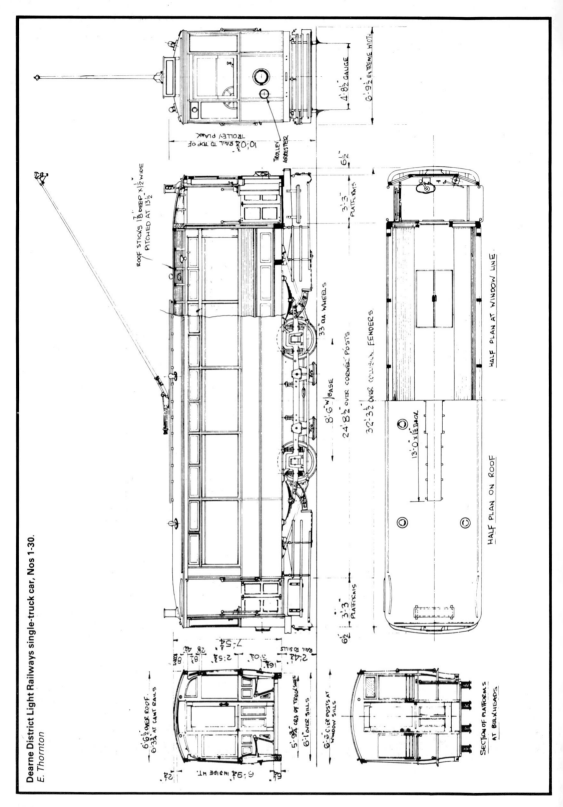

Dearne District Light Railways single-truck car, Nos 1-30.
E. Thornton

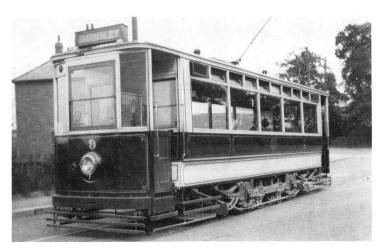

Dearne District No 9 at the Woodman terminus on 2 August 1931. Note the front exit door and P22 truck. *R. Elliott*

Sheffield or, as we have seen, by the introduction of specially designed 'lowbridge' cars, although this was not possible in the early days. In London long single-deck bogie cars were used on services through the Kingsway Subway until it was enlarged in 1931.

In a number of cases the Board of Trade (later Ministry of Transport) would not allow double-deck cars on routes involving steep hills, and in the early years there were a number of serious accidents as at Chatham and Huddersfield. Improvements in braking, especially the use of magnetic and air brakes, allowed double-deck cars to be used, but most systems retained single-deckers on hilly routes until abandonment. Examples include Hilltown via Constitution Road in Dundee and the Manchester Road, Summit, route in Burnley.

On light railways higher speeds were allowed if single-deck cars were used, and this was particularly important on inter-urban lines with little intermediate traffic, such as the Grimsby &

Immingham Light Railway built in 1913 by the Great Central Railway in connection with its new docks at Immingham. On the other hand the Portsdown & Horndean Light Railway used double-deck cars even though the line included Portsdown Hill and had many miles of track through what was then open country.

Small single-deck cars worked by one man were designed for those services where traffic no longer, or had never justified the use of the larger two-man cars. The first of the custom-built demi-cars, as they were called, was delivered to the Southport Tramways Co Ltd, another BET subsidiary, from Brush in 1903. Numbered 21, the car was 20ft long

Lowestoft Corporation owned four combination cars in its fleet of 19 passenger cars. Built by Milnes in 1903 and seating 50, they run on Milnes maximum traction bogies which tended to derail at passing loops.
Tramway & Railway World, courtesy J. H. Meridith

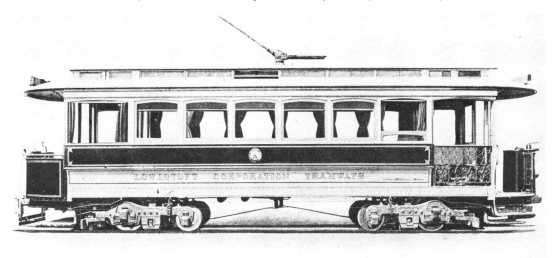

Maidstone demi-car No 18 in original condition at Barming. *Maidstone Corporation*

regenerative control, also patented by Raworth, and the savings in operating costs, especially wages and traction current, were considerable.

The success of the Southport experiment brought orders: two cars, Nos 9 and 10, were supplied to the Gravesend & Northfleet Co in 1904 and two others to Halifax Corporation. These cars had the original series-only controllers, but later demi-cars, probably starting with Chester No 13 in 1905, had the normal series-parallel type, and these were very successful.

The Gravesend demi-cars and some others had three side windows, but all except six built by Brush for Plymouth in 1906 had clerestory roofs.

Maidstone No 18, built by UEC in 1908, survived as a weekend bungalow at Winchelsea beach. It was rescued and is now in store. It is a classic – a diminutive fully-vestibuled four-window car with a seating capacity of 19, 15 in the saloon and two on each platform.

overall with a two-window saloon and a clerestory roof. It was mounted on a specially designed truck of 5ft wheelbase.

As the car was designed for one-man operation the platform entrances were reversed; passengers entered at the front and paid the driver, although a penny-in-the-slot system may have been used for a time. A folding step worked with an expanding gate closed the rear exit platform. The saloon seated 14 on cushioned longitudinal seats, and a further six, three on each platform, could sit on bench seats protected from the weather by a half vestibule. The car was designed by J. S. Raworth and the main technical innovation was his patented lifting bar which separated the driver's area and platform entrance from the passenger accommodation. The bar was locked to the controller through levers beneath the platform floor, so that when the bar was open to let passengers in or out the car could not be started. The car incorporated

---

Maidstone Corporation Light Railways No 18
Built: Preston 1909
Length overall: – 21ft 6in (over platforms)
Length over corner posts: – 11ft 0½in
Length of platforms: – 5ft 2in
Width over corner posts: – 6ft 2in
Seats: – 15: probably TW in saloon plus two on each platform (designed for six)
Trucks: – M&G 21E type; 5ft 6in wheelbase; 31in diameter wheels
Motors: – 2 Raworth
Controllers: – Raworth B series
Brakes: – Peacock hand wheel regenerative and track
Gauge: – 3ft 6in

Raworth's regenerative control system fell out of favour following an accident at Rawtenstall on 11 November 1911 when double-deck car No 14 ran out of control down Manchester Road, Accrington,

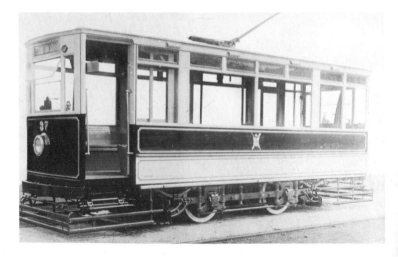

York No 37 – the last demi-car? It was built at Preston in 1924 after a deputation from the city had inspected the London United one-man cars. The front entrance-exit door was controlled by the driver. *Courtesy J. H. Price*

to collide with car No 11. Twenty passengers were injured and the resulting Board of Trade enquiry virtually ended regenerative control on tramways for the time being.

This, however, was not the end of the single-deck one-man car as there were still many lightly trafficked routes up and down the country. In the majority of cases single-deck cars were rebuilt from double-deckers with the stairs and top decks removed. Glasgow Corporation Tramways, for example, converted 120 horse trams for electric operation during 1899-1902 and a number of these saw further use. No 92 was rebuilt during May 1910 for the very short shuttle service on Finnieston Street, and when this was withdrawn transferred to

Llandudno single-deck cars

Above and below:
**The Llandudno & Colwyn Bay Electric Railway opened in 1907 with 14 large single-deck bogie cars built by the Midland Railway Carriage & Wagon Company. No 17 (ex-No 14) is on the Promenade at Rhos-on-Sea.
The four toast-racks from Preston in 1920, Nos 19-22, were popular with visitors on fine days. Here No 22 prepares to leave West Shore, Llandudno in August 1939.** *J. S. Webb*

the Paisley-Abbotsinch line which closed in May 1932. No 118, after serving as a parcels and ticket box car, was sold to the Luton Corporation Tramways in 1923. Re-numbered 13 it plied the

Rothesay Tramways Co Ltd could claim to have run the largest toast-rack tramcar. Rebuilt, if that's the word, from a 1902 Preston combination car, No 11 with seats for 80 passengers is on Rothesay Promenade. *D. L. G. Hunter*

Wardown route until the system closed in 1932. A further four of these cars (Nos 24, 32, 47 and 116) were sold to the Dumbarton Burgh & County Tramways in 1909. On this system they ran as single-deck cars (the stairs being closed off) on the Alexandra Fountain-Jamestown line where a low bridge in Bank Street, Alexandria, prevented the use of double-deckers.

One of the last one-man cars to be built was delivered from the Preston works in 1924 to the York Corporation Tramways. It was numbered 37 and with its quarter lights and air scoops looked like the lower saloon of a standard English Electric double-deck at first glance, but closer scrutiny revealed it to have a two-window saloon with enclosed flat-ended vestibuled platforms. The front entrance, on the nearside, had doors operated by a lever on the platform in conjunction with folding steps, and on each dash an illuminated sign announced 'Danger – Front Exit Car' when necessary. Roller blind destination screens were fitted at each end. The car was 25ft 6in long, had a Preston 21E type 6ft wheelbase truck, and controllers incorporating a 'deadman' device and airbrakes.

The car, however, had an unfortunate career; after being involved in two collisions it was used latterly as a sand and salt car.

Single-deck cars were used extensively on those lines built to serve or to create leisure facilities, as exemplified by the Manx Electric and Snaefell Mountain Railways. However, there were lines of similar character and I regret that I was never able to ride from Rothesay to Port Ballatine on the Isle of Bute or on the light railway from Stourbridge to Kinver. The course of the latter can still be traced today over 50 years after its closure, although bridges have been removed.

The tramways of most seaside resorts were worked by open-top double-deck cars of various types, but a number used open cross-bench or 'toast-rack' cars during the summer months. Examples included Blackpool, Southport, Llandudno, Southend and Weston-super-Mare, those at the latter two places being fitted with roofs.

The last traditional open 'toast-rack' trams were built in 1927 for Blackpool Corporation Tramways and brought that system's total to 32 of this type. Numbered 161-166, these last six had 13 full-width benches with reversible backs and seated 64 passengers, the trolley standard taking the place of the 65th passenger in the centre of the car. In 1936 the seating was reduced to 52 when a gangway

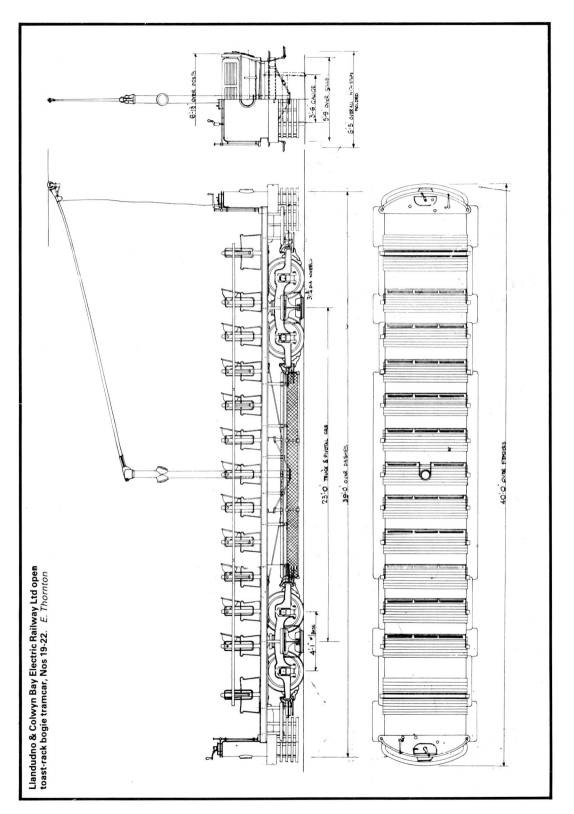

Llandudno & Colwyn Bay Electric Railway Ltd open toast-rack bogie tramcar, Nos 19-22. *E. Thornton*

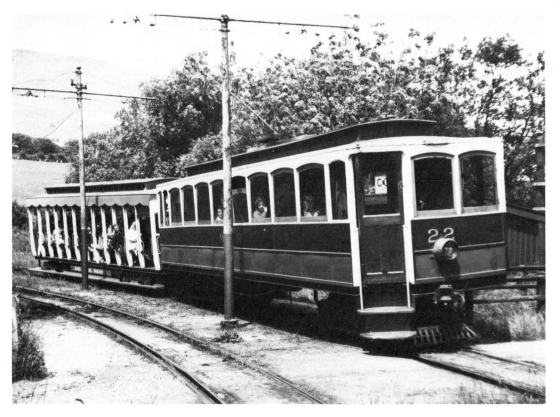

The typical motor car plus trailer operation on the Manx Electric Railway through service to Ramsey is epitomised by No 22 taking the corner at Cornaa on 11 June 1957.

was cut through the centre to provide conductor access when increasing motor traffic made it increasingly dangerous for him to move along the stepboards of the car from bench to bench.

These cars, consisting of little more than a floor with dashes at each end, were painted in a red livery, but this was later replaced by green for the dashes and white for the sideboards. They were used on the promenade and circular tour services until 1939 when the older cars of this type were scrapped.

Nos 161-166 were stored and in due course Nos 162 and 164 were broken up; No 161 became departmental car No 7 and for a time No 163 formed the base for the 'Blackpool Belle' illuminated car of 1959. The last two, Nos 165 and 166, were adapted as mobile television units and for 12 years toured and recorded the annual illuminations.

No 166 was presented to the Tramway Museum Society in 1972 and since that time has been restored, complete with full-width seats based on an original which survived the television unit era. The tram is extremely popular with visitors when the weather allows it to be used to the full.

The five Llandudno open toast-racks, Nos 19-23, were delivered from Preston in 1920 and survived to the closure of the system on the last days of

March 1956. These narrow-gauge cars could only seat four on each bench, but with 15 benches a total of 60 passengers could be carried; although they were more tightly packed than those on the Blackpool cars, I doubt if this aspect worried the holiday crowds.

The mainstay of the tramway service operated by the Rothesay Tramways Co Ltd (a BET subsidiary) from Rothesay to Ettrick Bay were long bogie single-deckers of the combination type built for the opening of the line in 1902. Nos 1-10 (Preston) and 16-20 (Brush in 1903) were roofed cross-bench cars with two end saloons, seating 50 passengers (32 plus 2×9 in each saloon). Nos 11-15 (Preston, 1902) had six window saloons in the centre and open compartments at each end, and they seated 46 passengers (30 in the saloon plus 2×8). The Preston cars had 22E bogies and the Brush cars Brush equal-wheel bogies; all had two trolley poles.

The last addition to the Rothesay fleet was demi-car No 21 transferred from the Greenock &

Llandudno & Colwyn Bay Electric Railway Ltd Nos 19-22
Built: Preston 1920
Length overall: – 40ft 0in
Width overall: – 6ft 5in with steps folded
Width over corner posts: – 6ft 1½in
Seats: – 60 TW
Trucks: – EE M&G type equal wheel bogies; 4ft 1in
wheelbase; 31¾in diameter wheels
Motors: – 2 x GE 249; 25hp
Controllers: – B18 DD
Brakes: – Hand wheel, magnetic track
Gauge: – 3ft 6in

Manx Electric Railway Nos 1-2
Built: Birkenhead 1893
Length overall: – 34ft 9in
Width overall: – 6ft 6in
Height to trolley plank: – 11ft 2in
Seats (saloon): – 38 LW
Trucks: – Brush type D
Motors: – 4 x Soc, L'E et H, Charleroi, TIIA; 25hp
Brakes: – Hand wheel, air
Gauge: – 3ft 0in

Nos 11 and 12, were rebuilt as open toast-racks
seating 80 passengers on 16 full-width benches;
the trolley standard was presumably fitted between
the central benches. It would seem that Rothesay
could claim to have run both the smallest and
largest open toast-rack cars in the British Isles.
Originally painted red and white and later blue and
white they must have created a fine sight as they
made their way along the coast and across to the
other side of the island.

Fortunately it is still possible to travel along the

Manx Electric Railway Nos 19-22
Built: Birkenhead 1899
Length overall: – 37ft 6in
Width overall: – 7ft 4in
Height to trolley plank: – 11ft 0in
Seats: – 48 TW in two saloons
Trucks: – Brill 27G
Motors: – 4 x Soc L'E et H, Charleroi, TIIA; 25hp
Brakes: – Hand wheel, air
Gauge: – 3ft 0in

Port Glasgow Co (another BET subsidiary) c1924.
This car was rebuilt as an open toast-rack c1928
and seated 45 on nine transverse seats, only one
less than the longer Brush bogie cars.

Open toast-racks were obviously popular on this
seaside line, because two of the Preston 1902 cars,

'Lye' single-deck No 1 in the Tividale Works yard when new
in February 1915. The cars seated 16 in each compartment
and had long-wheelbase 8ft 6in trucks probably constructed
at Tividale. The narrowness of the ventilators and the flat
roof can be seen clearly. *Birmingham & Midland Joint
Tramways, courtesy J. S. Webb*

coast in an open-sided tram, but to do so we have to cross over to the Isle of Man where roofed toast-racks and vintage saloon cars operate an intensive service from Douglas (Derby Castle) to Laxey during the summer season. The oldest of these cars were built by G. F. Milnes & Co for the opening of the line in 1893. Numbered 1 and 2 they are long unvestibuled saloons standing high off the ground and now running on Brush bogies. Six more cars were delivered from the same manufacturers in 1894 and were generally similar in appearance but with vestibuled driving platforms. Nos 5, 6, 7 and 9 of this series are still extant, whereas Nos 4 and 8 together with No 3, an original car, were destroyed by fire in 1930. Nos 19-22 are the winter saloons built in 1899 and nos

Below:
Brush-built open combination car No 49 with toast-rack centre section in the woods near Kinver depot. It is shown with trucks in the normal position; note the turtle-back roof and the two trolleys.
The late James Nelson, courtesy J. S. Webb

Manx Electric Railway – Motor cars

Nos	Date	Builder	Remarks
1-2	1893	G. F. Milnes	Unvestibuled saloons; 12 windows; 38 seats, longitudinal; Brush bogies.
6,7,9	1894	G. F. Milnes	Vestibuled saloons; 12 windows; 36 seats, longitudinal cushioned; Brush bogies
5		G. F. Milnes	As 6, 7 and 9 but with 32 transverse seats.
14-18	1898	G. F. Milnes	Cross-bench with shutters, 56 seats (10 benches plus four each side of bulkhead); Brush bogies (No 16 Milnes).
19-22	1899	G. F. Milnes	Winter saloons; eight windows; 48 seats, transverse; Brill bogies.
25-27	1898	G. F. Milnes	As Nos 14-18; originally trailers, with Brush bogies.
28-31	1904	UEC	Cross-bench trailers; 56 seats.
32-33	1906	UEC	Cross-bench trailers; 56 seats.

Handwritten on photograph: *Knows... ory Closed type carry 52 passrs.*

Brush 'Cradley Bogie' No 56 in original condition in Dunsley Meadows near Stourton. The ventilators of the clerestory roof can be compared with those of the turtle-back design on No 49. *The late A. Jensen, courtesy J. S. Webb*

14-18 and 25-33 cross-bench cars, of which Nos 25-27 were originally delivered unmotored and used as trailers until motorised in 1903. They were built by Milnes in 1898, except for the Nos 28-33 bought from Preston in 1904 and 1906.

There are also 25 trailers, numbered between 36 and 62, of which Nos 57-59 are saloons and the remainder roofed cross-bench cars mostly with roller shutters, seating 44 passengers. The exception is No 52, now a flat truck used for carrying rails and other material and usually to be seen parked at Dhoon quarry siding. The oldest were also built by G. F. Milnes, but the later ones,

including three replacements built in 1930 to the original design, are from Preston.

The basic service is operated by saloon cars with or without one of the newer trailers, but in the season when extra cars are 'run as required by traffic' cross-bench motor and trailer sets work to Laxey and occasionally to Ramsey.

Dudley, Stourbridge & District Electric Traction Co Ltd

	Built: Nos 1-18 Loughborough 1899	Nos 19-25, Preston 1900
Length overall:	– 28ft 3½in	27ft 2in
Length over corner posts:	– 19ft 4in	18ft 2in
Length of centre compartment:	– 11ft 9in	11ft 9in
Length of platforms:	– 4ft 0in	4ft 0in
Width overall:	– 6ft 0in	6ft 2in
Height to trolley plank:	– 9ft 10in	11ft 0in
Height to saloon roof:	– 7ft 0in	7ft 10½in to monitor
Seats (saloon):	– 16 LW	26 LW
Seats (end compartments):	– 6 LW	
Trucks:	– Peckham Cantilever 8B or Brush 'Peckham' 6ft 6in wheelbase	'Lord Baltimore' 6ft 6in wheelbase
Motors:	– 2 x GE 800 25hp	2 x GE 800 25hp
Controllers:	– BTH K2	BTH K2
Brakes:	– Hand, emergency,	Slipper, hand, emergency

At Laxey there is a connection to the Snaefell Mountain Railway. This line is worked by six cars, Nos 1-6, built by G. F. Milnes for the opening of the line in 1895. All these cars now have modern equipment and No 5 a replica body built at Ramsey.

A ride on the Manx Electric Railway is a must for anyone wishing to sample tramway nostalgia in addition to breathtaking views of sea and coast. The majority of the rolling stock is over 80 years old and, although there is variation in detailed design, they were built to last: their polished wood reflects the cheerful holiday-makers who have ridden in them over the years.

As noted earlier the largest exclusive user of single deck cars was the Potteries Electric Traction Co Ltd, a BET subsidiary, with 115 cars all replaced by single-deck buses during 1926-27. The BET also built up a large network of tramways in the West Midlands through its subsidiary companies. Although the trunk routes to Birmingham, via West Bromwich or Oldbury, were operated by double-deck cars, many of the local services,

---

Dudley, Stourbridge & District Electric Traction Co Ltd
Built: Nos 6, 21, 32, 70 Tividale 1916
Length overall: – 44ft 9in
Length over corner posts: – 37ft 9in
Length of centre compartment: – 15ft 9in
Length of platform: – 3ft 0in
Width overall: – 6ft 6in
Width over corner posts: – 6ft 0in
Height to trolley plank: – 10ft 6in
Height to saloon roof: – 7ft 3in
Seats (centre compartment): – 24 TW
Seats (end compartments): – 16 LW each
Trucks: – Brush D equal wheel bogies
Motors: – 2 x GE 60; 35hp
Controllers: – BTH K 10
Brakes: – Hand, emergency, Spencer slipper

Tividale front exit car No 4 at Kingswinford on the last day of Dudley-Kingswinford services, on 31 December 1925.
S. Kelding, courtesy J. S. Webb

last Tram to run between Kingswinford and Dudley
(Photo. Skelding, Summer St, Kingswinf

Dudley, Stourbridge & District Electric Traction Co Ltd

Nos 49-51 Loughborough 1902	Nos 52-59 Loughborough 1902
Length overall: – 44ft 6½in	44ft 8in
Length over corner posts: – 37ft 7½in	35ft 4½in
Length of centre compartment: – 21ft 1½in	21ft 11in
Length of platforms: – 3ft 0in	3ft 9in
Width overall: – 6ft 5½in	6ft 0in
Width over corner posts: – 6ft 0in	6ft 0in
Height to trolley plank: – 10ft 9in	10ft 10in
Height to saloon roof: – 7ft 3in	7ft 6in to clerestory
Seats (centre section): – 32 on 8 benches	32 LW
Seats (end sections): – 12 LW each	10LW each
Trucks: – Brush Rev MaxT bogies; later normal MaxT	Brush D equal wheel bogies
Motors: – 2 x Brush 1000A, 25hp	4 x GE 60, 25hp*
Controllers: – Brush HD 2	Brush K 12
Brakes: – Hand, Rheostatic	Hand, emergency, slipper.

* Nos 57, 59 had Brush 1000D type

including the lengthy rural line to Kinver, were worked by a variety of single-deckers.

On a double-deck car smokers could be accommodated on the open upper deck, but as this was not possible on a single-deck vehicle the passenger area would often be divided into two or more compartments.

The Dudley, Stourbridge & District Electric Traction Co Ltd opened its main line from Dudley to Stourbridge on 26 July 1899 with nine cars from the Brush Co. These small cars had a three-window central saloon separated from the two smoking compartments (which were open to the platforms) by bulkheads with sliding doors. The five fixed side windows were of the Brush 'curved top' type with ventilation through opening lights fixed in the shallow clerestory of the turtle back roof. These nine cars had American-built Peckham cantilever Type 8B trucks, but Nos 10-18 which followed had Brush-built trucks of the Peckham type.

The next batch of cars were part of a bulk order placed by the BET with the Preston works. Numbered 19-25 and 43-45 (Nos 43-45 were originally Kinver cars Nos 1-3) in the fleet they had five framed drop windows with square tops and a full-length clerestory roof with ventilators. They seated 26 passengers in the one saloon and were mounted on American-built 'Lord Baltimore' trucks.

Marketed as the 'Improved Preston single deck type', these cars were evidently not very popular with the management and together with the Brush cars had been scrapped, rebuilt as double-deck or converted to other uses by 1920. One reason for this would have been their low seating capacity and the use of double-deck cars on the main Dudley-Stourbridge line.

To replace the original Brush cars on the Stourbridge-Lye service four new cars, numbered 1, 2, 7 and 10 (ii) were built in 1915 at the Tividale works, opened in 1907 to service the tramways

operated by the Birmingham & Midland Tramways Joint Committee. The new cars had to pass under a very low bridge at Stourbridge Town station (still extant) and had an overall height of 10ft 5in and, even then, the trolley pole had to be bent to fit! They were vestibuled four-window, two-compartment cars with narrow ventilators above the windows and an almost flat roof. Two similar cars were built for the Birmingham District's Spon Lane and Bromford Lane lines at the same time.

One solution to the problem of capacity on those routes restricted to single-deck operation, especially the Kinver Light Railway, was the introduction of exceptionally long bogie cars. Eleven were obtained from the Brush Co in 1902 and a further four built at Tividale in 1916.

The first three Brush cars, later Nos 49-51, originally built for the Kinver Light Railway and the second batch of cars to be numbered 1-3, replaced the three 'Preston' cars which opened the line on 5 April 1901. Built on a one-level steel underframe these cars had two end saloons seating 12 each on longitudinal benches and an open centre section which seated 32 on eight full-width benches. The cars had the, by then, old-fashioned 'turtle back' roof, but no ventilation was required as all the windows were unglazed, although glazed bulkheads, as on the Manx Electric cars, separated the drivers platform from the passenger accommodation, and cut down draughts to some extent. In later years a gangway was cut through the centre benches, and doors provided in the bulkheads, to allow the conductor to walk through the car rather than along the step boards.

The other Brush cars, Nos 52-59, had three-compartment, clerestory-roofed saloons with the traditional Brush curved window tops. The no-smoking five-window centre compartment was separated from the two smoking compartments by sliding doors, but the latter were open to the platforms; outside hung doors were fitted later. These vehicles replaced the small cars on the Cradley Heath route, but as Kinver specials were to be seen operating over a large part of the system. Known as Cradley bogies they were rebuilt during 1924-25 as front exit cars. They were also fitted with doors and vestibuled. Other improvements included cushioned seats, arm rests (except for the first two rebuilds, Nos 52 and 54) and panelled ceilings painted cream. It's a pity they were only to run for another four or five years at the most.

Four longer cars, Nos 6, 21, 32 and 70, were built at Tividale in 1916. The one-level steel underframe was presumably similar to those used for Nos 49-51 but the body design was unique and particularly suited to the Kinver Light Railway and the variable local climate. There were the usual three compartments and vestibuled driving platforms, but no bulkheads at all – the necessary strength being given by arched transoms with side support.

The central compartment seated 24 on transverse benches divided by a central gangway, and in wet weather three of the four open doorways on each side could be closed by fitting in panel sections which were normally stored at the depot. The two end compartments had four glazed rounded-top windows and seated 16 each on longitudinal seats. To allow clearance for the Brush equal wheel bogies the cars were high off the ground. This caused difficulties for passengers boarding and alighting so that extra steps had to be fitted.

Meantime the Tividale works had evolved a 'standard' double-deck open-canopy four-window single-truck car, and at least 14 were built between 1913 and 1917, including four in open-top form: two were for Dudley, Stourbridge, and two for the Worcester Electric Tramways Co Ltd.

The need to replace the older rolling stock was becoming urgent and so Richard Humphries, the Birmingham & Midland Tramways Joint Commit-

tee's engineer, designed a basic single-deck car which was cheap to build, less wearing on the track and fully enclosed. The prototype car, No 2 in the South Staffordshire Tramways' fleet, appeared in 1917 and there were a number of new features. It was of front exit design and built without bulkheads, although the conventional underframe with dropped platforms was used. To give strength, as in the 1916 bogie cars, stiffening transoms were fitted at each end of the passenger compartment; a further stiffener, across the roof only at the centre, held the car's sides together and gave support to the trolley plank.

The body was of the traditional wooden construction with waist and rocker panels although the latter was only slightly concave. The six side windows had the older style curved tops, possibly because the patterns used for repairs were readily available. The only ventilation was from the six air scoops in the cant rail and an opening window on the nearside of each vestibule. Ventilation, however, soon proved inadequate and in an attempt to overcome the problem an opening sash at the top of one window on each side was fitted. In the production cars, and later on No 2, similar opening sashes were fitted to all the side windows and the driver was given an opening vent at the top of his windscreen.

Another noteworthy feature of the new car was the doors: the front exit door under the control of the driver opened outward while the entrance door opened inwards, but sliding entrance doors were fitted to all production cars.

The interior was austere by modern standards with ribbed roof and longitudinal wooden seats for 32 passengers, but there was standing room for many more down the centre of the car and on the platforms.

The car was successful and by the end of 1920 over 30, including one for the Potteries, had been built at Tividale. They were Nos 101-110 and others taking the numbers of withdrawn cars. A further 10, Nos 71-80 to the same design, were built at Loughborough. The design was copied by Wolverhampton Corporation and Barrow-in-Furness, and also adapted by the Gateshead Co for its new and rebuilt cars.

Passengers comfort was improved in later years when cushions were fitted to the seats, and later cars had armrests, 15 on each side; but these vehicles were not really large enough to cope with the traffic on the busier routes and a number found their way on to the Kinver line. For this summer traffic the cars had opening frames fitted to the side windows: with these frames fastened on to the body sides, and being to all intents open cars, they would sway gently across the fields and through the woods to Kinver, a swansong to the variety of cars that had gone that way before them.

Birmingham & Midland Tramways Joint Committee
Built: No 2 Prototype Front Exit 1917
Length overall: – 33ft 2¾in
Length over corner posts: – 21ft 8¾in
Length of platforms: – 5ft 3in
Width overall: – 6ft 6in
Height to trolley plank: – 10ft 2in
Height to saloon roof: – 6ft 11in
Seats (saloon): – 32 LW; later cushioned
Trucks: – Tividale 8ft 6in, wheelbase; some production cars had Brill 21E wide wing type
Motors: – 2 x GE249A; 40hp
Controllers: – BTH B.18
Brakes: – Hand, rheostatic; some production cars fitted with magnetic track for hills

6. The Major Cities

London

By 1950, when the conversion of the surviving London tramways to bus operation restarted, the rolling stock had become very standardised, in great contrast to the position in 1933 when the London Passenger Transport Board was formed. On 1 July of that year 2,630 tramcars from 11 different operators (eight municipal and three company owned) passed to the newly formed Board. By far the largest of these fleets was that of the LCC Tramways with 1,713 cars, followed by the Metropolitan and London United companies with 316 and 150 respectively. The other municipal owners contributed 399 and the South Metropolitan Co a further 52.

Although the larger undertakings, especially the LCC, had standardised fleets, there was an immense variety of tramcar within the London area. These ranged from the older bogie and single-truck cars dating from the start of electric tramway operation to the modern luxury tramcars built a few years previously. They were nearly all built by the outside firms, but the larger undertakings submitted their own designs and so developed distinctive styles, with the large bogie car dominating the London area.

London United Tramways was first in the field with electric traction. (The first line was the Alexandra Park Electric Railway opened on 13 May 1898 with four tramcars. It closed on 30 September 1899 after two seasons of operation. The Metropolitan opened two lines to Alexandra Place in 1905 and 1906 which were closed by London Transport in 1938.) The first regular electric tramcar service opened on 4 May 1901, and initially services were from Shepherds Bush to Acton, Shepherd Bush to Kew Bridge and Hammersmith to Kew Bridge. The London United Co, under the energetic leadership of Sir Clifton Robinson, was an ambitious company but the network never reached the extent envisaged and almost throughout its life there was a surplus of rolling stock. The initial order was for 300 open-top bogie cars and these were built by Hurst Nelson, Milnes and BEC.

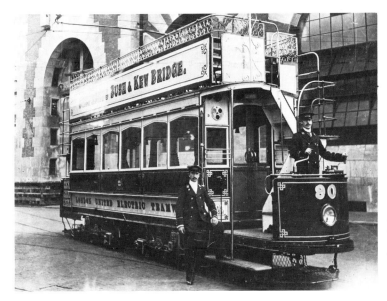

The London United Electric Tramways had a fleet of 300 identical six-window bogie tramcars with 'broken' staircases: No 80, when new, is posed outside Chiswick depot.
London Regional Transport

London United Tramways Type U Nos 251-275
Built: Hadley 1902
Length overall: – 33ft 0in
Length over corner posts: – 22ft 0in
Width over corner posts: – 6ft 0in (over sills)
Height to trolley plank: – 16ft 0in when top covered
Stairs: – Broken or landing
Seats (lower saloon): – 30 LW
Seats (upper saloon): – 40 TW 2+2
Trucks: – Brill 22E bogies
Motors: – 2 x Westinghouse 49B (c1933)
Controllers: – Westinghouse 90 (c1933)
Brakes: – Hand wheel, rheostatic, magnetic

London United Tramways Type T Nos 301-340
Built: Preston 1906
Length overall: – 34ft 7½in
Width overall: – 7ft 2in
Height to trolley plank: – 15ft 10in
Stairs: – Broken or landing
Seats (lower saloon): – 30 LW; later TU
Seats (upper saloon): – 44 TW 2+2
Trucks: – Brill bogies
Motors: – 2 x Westinghouse; 40hp, later MV 60hp
Brakes: – Hand wheel, rheostatic

Built to specifications drawn up by the LUT engineers, they had six-window saloons, monitor ceilings, longitudinal seating and completely open platforms. Their main distinguishing feature was the 'broken' staircase with the two sections at right angles separated by a landing. About 100 of these cars were later top-covered and a fair number, re-equipped with 50 or 60hp motors, survived to operate in London Transport colours.

A further 40 cars, Nos 301-340, were supplied by UEC in 1906. These were top-covered and built to the more modern design with opening quarter lights, but they retained the 'broken' staircase. These cars had more powerful motors of 40hp and after a short stay in the Kingston area were transferred to the Uxbridge trunk route until, in their turn, they were superseded by the 'Felthams'.

The London United tramcars were vehicles of quality with a high standard of finish both inside and out. The saloon was entered by double doors, and inside the ornate roof style, cushioned seats, curtains and fancy lightshades gave it a luxury look. The first cars appeared in a red and white livery, but others were painted all white or blue and white, although, in time, the red and white colour scheme became standard.

The Metropolitan Electric Tramways Ltd, opened its first electric routes comparatively late, on 22 July 1904, from Finsbury Park to Wood Green and to Tottenham (Seven Sisters Corner). By February 1911 the system had reached its full extent with lines to Acton, Sudbury, Canons Park, Barnet, Enfield and Wood Green, a total of 53.51 route miles (84km) of which it owned a mere 9.38 miles (14.5km). The remainder was owned by the Middlesex County Council, 42.63 miles (67km), and the Hertfordshire County Council, 1.5 miles (3km), and operated under lease.

This caused complications because the type of rolling stock had to be agreed with the councils and, as a BET associated company had to be purchased from the Brush Co. The Middlesex Council favoured the London United 'broken stair' design and as a result 60 of the first 150 cars (Type A Nos 71-130) were so built, while the company cars (Type B Nos 1-70) were more orthodox in design with canopies and direct half-turn stairs. The six side windows had drop sashes with inward opening lights above. The two inner windows were larger than the others and the cars similar to LCC classes A and D.

Unusually the lower saloon seating varied in the

Many of the London United Tramcars seen in the previous illustration, including No 268, were later fitted with matching top covers. *Real Photographs*

The 40 Class T cars from Preston which followed in 1906 were of more modern design but retained the 'broken' staircase. No 327 is seen as delivered with airscoops. *London Regional Transport*

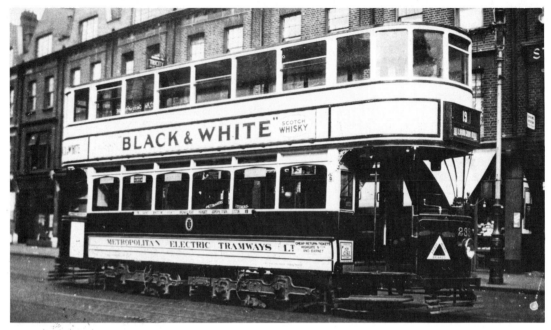

Metropolitan Electric Tramways Type H Nos 237-316
Built: Loughborough 1909-12
Length overall: – 35ft 0in
Length over corner posts: – 22ft 2in
Width overall: – 7ft 1in
Width over corner posts: – 6ft 0½in
Height to trolley plank: – 15ft 5⅝in
Stairs: – Direct 90°
Seats (lower saloon): – 32 LW Rattan; later TU 2+1
Seats (upper saloon): – 46 TW 2+2
Trucks: – Brush LCC MaxT type (Nos 237-241 had M&G 3L bogies)
Motors: – 2 x GE 67; 40 hp. 2 x BTH 509; 60hp when remotored
Controller: – BTH B49
Brakes: – Hand wheel, rheostatic, magnetic

The Metropolitan Electric Tramways had a much more varied fleet. Class G cars with 'Tudor Arch' windows and open top decks were later top-covered, while the Class H cars which followed were top covered from the outset. This is No 233 of Class G at Euston terminus in 1929. *R. Elliott*

Type B cars. Nos 1-35 had longitudinal wood strip seats like the LCC cars, but Nos 36-70 had staggered transverse 2+1 seats with woven rattan covers for 24 passengers. By 1918 the transverse had been replaced by longitudinal seating for 30. Both types had wooden 2+2 transverse seats on the upper deck.

The Council, with the usual civic pride of the period, also favoured the monitor roof and so all

Bluebell, No 318, combined lightweight construction techniques with high passenger capacity. Built in 1927, its appearance was much improved by the addition of a domed roof, as displayed by the car at North Finchley on 9 June 1935.
Newham Libraries HCVC collection

further cars, up to No 216, had this feature, including the last five cars of Type F which were built with top covers. All the monitor roof cars had the 'Tudor Arch' style of side window and this style was perpetuated in the later cars, even though they had plain ceilings and opening lights. These later cars, Type G Nos 217-236 and Type H Nos 237-316, were built by Brush between 1909 and 1912 with fully enclosed top decks, except for Type G cars which received them later.

Type E cars (Nos 131-150 for the record) were single-deck cars with flat top windows and clerestory roofs for the Alexandra Palace lines.

Although some Type B cars received top covers and new 40hp motors during 1913-15 and were designated Type B2, and many experiments were tried during the 1920s, it was not until 1926 that the programme to improve rolling stock and speed up services got under way. The first was achieved by fitting 2+1 upholstered transverse seats to all cars of types C1, G and H, and moquette covered cushions on the longitudinal seats of types A and C2. Driver's windscreens were also fitted to all G and H type cars. Most of the cars were re-equipped with new 50 and 60hp BTH 509 motors to make them the fastest in the London area.

The problem of obsolete rolling stock, especially on the trunk routes, was becoming more acute as the speed and comfort of the competing omnibuses improved. The Companies, part of the 'Underground Group' since 1912, set their engineers the task of producing a tramcar that could match, and beat, the rival for both speed and comfort.

The engineers set about their task with enthusiasm and to try out their new ideas a number of experimental cars were built. The first two, known as *Poppy* (LUT No350) and *Bluebell* (MET No 318) after their striking new colour schemes, entered service during 1927. *Poppy,* with its domed driving cabins extending out at each end, and with a passing resemblence to the NS bus of the period, has been described as 'the most ungainly tramcar ever constructed', while *Bluebell* (which reminded me of the upper structure of a Mississippi stern wheeler), was much improved by the addition of a domed roof during 1928.

The companies had been experimenting with passenger flow at this time and the two cars were of the rear entrance/front exit design with air operated platform doors. *Bluebell* was the more important of the two as it combined light weight construction (ash framing with aluminium panels) with a high carrying capacity (71 seated + 34 standing).

Passenger comfort was greatly improved in the new 'Feltham' cars: this is a lower saloon.
London Regional Transport

**London United Tramways Type UCC Nos 351-396,
Metropolitan Electric Tramways Type UCC Nos 319,
321-329, 332-375**
Built: Feltham 1931
Length overall: – 40ft 10in
Width overall: – 7ft 1¾in tapering to 6ft 11¼in
Height to trolley plank: – 15ft 11in
Height inside lower saloon: – 6ft 2¾in
Height inside upper saloon: – 5ft 11in
Stairs: – Straight, 90° turn at bottom
Seats (lower saloon): – 22 TU 2+2 moquette
Seats (upper saloon): – 42 TU 2+2 moquette
Trucks: – EE MaxT (LUT), EMB MaxT (MET); 4ft 6in
wheelbase
Motors: – 2 x GEC WT29 (LUT), 2 x BTH 509 P1 (MET); 70hp
Controllers: – KB5 (LUT), OK33B (MET)
Brakes: – Hand wheel, air wheel, magnetic

There is no doubt that the experience gained with *Poppy* and *Bluebell* was incorporated in the next three cars. The prototype 'Felthams' were built by The Union Construction & Finance Co (an Underground subsidiary set up to build underground rolling stock) at Feltham, Middlesex in 1929 and 1930 for the MET. They were No 320 on equal wheel bogies, No 330 on maximum traction bogies and No 331, a centre-entrance design, again on equal wheel bogies. The first two were also equipped for 'Pay as you enter' fare collection, but this led to delays in service and was not perpetuated.

The 100 production 'Felthams' were built during 1931 and incorporated all the best features from the prototype cars. Described as 'magnificent' and as 'ahead of their time', these cars certainly brought a new dimension of speed and comfort to the London transport scene.

The main features of the new cars were their length, tapering body and the large entrance/exit vestibules with double folding entrance doors and a sliding air operated exit door under the control of the driver. The floor height was lower than on traditional cars and because of this, and unlike the earlier experimental cars, the cabs were raised above saloon window level. This brought the seated driver's eye to the same level as his colleagues who still had to stand.

Each vestibule had room for 10 standing passengers and a seat on the near side for the conductor, assuming he could find time to sit on it! There were four windows with inward opening lights to the lower saloon, and composite construction combined with the thin metal sheeting allowed more room for passenger comfort.

After a 90° turn from the platform, straight stairs led directly to the upper saloon which was open throughout its length and very spacious. At each end a curved seat for five faced inwards, and a straight seat for four more faced the stairhead. All seating was in moquette. The upper saloon had half drop windows and ceilings were painted white, but surprisingly the lights, although recessed, were not fitted with shades. It probably made cleaning and replacement easier.

The 'Felthams' were also equipped for speed and comfort. Two 70hp motors, together with roller bearing axleboxes, could accelerate the 18-ton tramcar to a speed of 20mph in 20 seconds. They served Londoners well; first to Uxbridge, Wood Green and Finchley; and later to Streatham, Tooting, Croydon and Purley.

Fleet Numbers
Experimental: MET Nos 318, 320, 330, 331; LUT No 350; LPTB Nos 2255, 2166-2168, 2317.
Felthams: MET Nos 319, 321-329, 332-375; LUT Nos 351-396; LPTB Nos 2066-2119, 2120-2165.

Similar comfort was also offered by LCC No 1 – the upper saloon shows the tapering sides and enclosed lighting.
London Regional Transport

London Transport 1931 Union Construction & Finance Co
'Feltham' car. *E. Thornton*

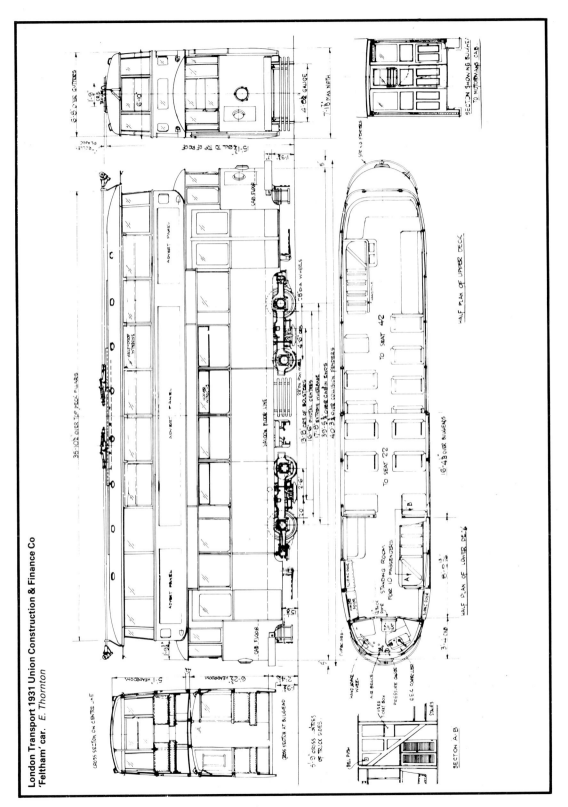

The Feltham tramcars were latterly used in South London: No 2165 was at Clapham Common on route 20 on 10 June 1949. On non-standard bogies, this car was rarely in service. *J. H. Meredith*

The London County Council commenced to operate horse tramways on 1 January 1899 when it took over all the lines of the London Tramways Co. Acquisitions had begun in 1895 and although nearly all the lines in the County had been taken over by 1909 the process was not completed until 1922. The first electric LCC tram ran on 1 May 1903 and the electrification of the horse tramways, except for some short lines which were abandoned, was completed on 28 July 1921 when the Hackney-West India Dock line re-opened.

The LCC fleet was highly standardised, and, following the initial deliveries of 400 open-top cars, a policy of top-covering was decided upon which, in the case of the bogie cars (Classes A and D), increased seating capacity from 66 to 74.

The County's policy of cheap workmen's fares together with rehousing in the suburbs led to a tremendous growth in peak hour traffic and to meet this need the LCC engineers designed a large capacity bogie car that was to serve Londoners for years to come – 45 in fact!

The result was the introduction in 1906 of the 'E' class, the first cars in London with enclosed top decks. These were so successful that after 300 had been built an improved version, the E1, appeared in 1907, and this class eventually totalled 1,050 units. Cars to this design were also supplied to East Ham, Walthamstow, West Ham and Croydon.

Although Hurst Nelson and Brush built most of these cars, a considerable number were constructed at the old Leytonstone works of the North Metropolitan Tramways, then leased to the LCC Tramways. These included No 1025, now at

London County Council Tramways Class E1*
Built: 1907-22
Length overall: – 33ft 10in
Length over corner posts: – 22ft 2in
Length of platform: – 5ft 10in
Width overall: – 7ft 2in
Height to trolley plank: – 15ft 9¾in
Height inside lower saloon: – 6ft 2¾in
Height inside upper saloon: – 6ft 1¾in
Stairs: – Direct 90°
Seats (lower saloon): – 32 LW; later 27 TU 2+1
Seats (upper saloon): – 46 TW 2+2
Trucks: – M&G MaxT; 4ft 6in wheelbase; 31¾in/21¾in diameter wheels
Brakes: – Hand wheel, magnetic track

* 'E1' class: Nos 752-1426 Hurst Nelson/LCC, 1907-10: Nos 1477-1676 Brush 1910-13: Nos 1727-1776, 1777-1851 Hurst Nelson 1920-22, Nos 552-601 metal top decks, equipment ex-Kingsway subway cars
'E' class: 402-551, 602-751 Hurst Nelson UEC 1907
'M' class: 1427-1476, 1677-1726 Hurst Nelson

the Covent Garden Museum, which is fitted with Hurst Nelson trucks and equipment.

The E1 tramcar was slightly larger than the E and was of traditional 'Rocker Panel' construction with bulkheads and four large saloon windows. In the lower saloon ventilation was by side opening lights and seating initially wooden and longitudinal.

Half-turn stairs gave access to the upper deck through a stairhead door. London tramcars built before 1931 had no windscreens (police regulations) and the staircase was screened off from the upper deck to prevent draughts. The upper deck was spartan with framed drop windows, a wood 'plank' ceiling and cramped wooden seating, especially in the canopies. The windows were connected by rods and wound up and down by a ratchet opposite the front stairhead.

All the E1 cars had LCC Class 4 maximum traction 'swing bolster' trucks especially designed to support a heavy double-deck car. Equipped with magnetic track brakes a high scheduled speed could be maintained, especially by the later cars fitted with 60hp motors. These included Nos 1727-1851 of 1921 which were based at Clapham depot for many years. They were so lively that in many cases their bodies were later braced with diagonal tie-bars to hold them together!

The LCC also had to face up to intensive omnibus competition and it met this with the 'Pullman' programme of renovation. Between 1926 and 1929 most E1 cars were fitted with comfortable upholstered transverse seating on the lower decks, and seating capacity was reduced from 78 to 73. They were painted in a new red livery in place of the traditional chocolate and by 1933 the new livery was applied to all LCC cars then extant.

In 1919 the LCC considered new designs but the E2 never got beyond the drawing board. It has been said that E1 No 1235 was rebuilt with a front

exit and other minor modifications (eg inset indicator blinds)., as Class E2, but it was not a success and quickly converted back again. It was not until 1930 that two new prototype cars, No 1852 Class HR1 and No 1853 with an all-metal body, were built at Charlton works. A total of 260 cars to this new design, Classes HR2 and E3, were built by Hurst Nelson and English Electric by the end of 1931.

London County Council Tramways, Class E3 and HR2*
Built: 1930-31
Length overall: – 33ft 10in
Length over corner posts: – 22ft 2in
Length of platforms: – 5ft 10in
Width overall: – 7ft 1in
Height to trolley plank: – 15ft 7in to top of roof
Stairs: – Direct 90°
Seats (lower saloon): – 28 TU 2+2
Seats (upper saloon): – 46 TU 2+2
Trucks: – EMB MaxT 4ft 9in wheelbase ('E3'); EMB equal wheel 4ft 6in wheelbase ('HR2')
Brakes: – Hand wheel, magnetic track. 'HR2' also had electric run back brake

* 'E3' class: Nos 1904-2003 Hurst Nelson 1930-31; 161-210 English Electric 1930-31 (for Leyton Council)
'HR1' class: No1852 LCC 1930
'HR2' class: No 1853 LCC; Nos 1854-1903 English Electric 1930; Nos 101-160 Hurst Nelson 1930-31

The LCC 'E' class car of 1906, represented here by No 734 at Stamford Hill, was a very successful high capacity bogie car and the forerunner of a large fleet. *W. A. Camwell*

Standard 1920 type LCC 'E1' car. *E. Thornton*

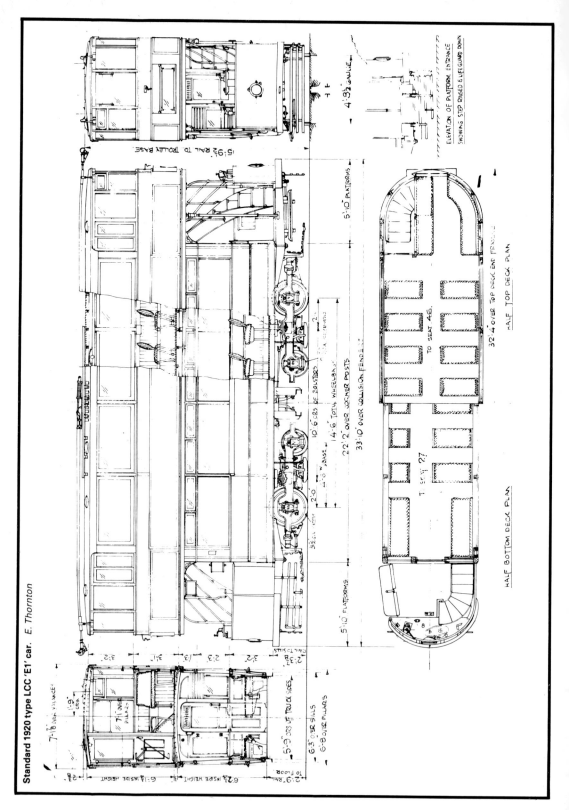

HALF BOTTOM DECK PLAN

HALF TOP DECK PLAN

ELEVATION OF PLATFORM ENTRANCE

SHOWING STEP RAISED & LIFEGUARD DOWN

The HR2 cars with four motors and equal-wheel bogies were for the hilly routes via Dulwich (Dog Kennel Hill) and to Highgate Village, and replaced the ageing four-wheeled 'M' class. In addition to the hand and magnetic brakes the HR2s had a special electric runback brake for extra safety. All cars previously used on the hilly routes had a track brake, operated by hand and applied by turning a wheel mounted on the handbrake staff. The four-wheelers used on Highgate Hill had a brake which screwed down and clamped above and below the conduit slot. It was applied by a brakesman who boarded at the 'Archway Tavern' and rode up the hill and back.

The E3s were all metal cars on maximum traction bogies for the new subway routes and the Leyton area. The Leyton tramways had been operated by the LCC since 1 July 1921 and 50 of the new cars were owned by Leyton Borough Council.

These handsome cars were built on traditional lines, and compared with the 'Felthams' built at the same time, were out of date, at least in appearance. However on their modern EMB bogies, and with less cramped seating, they were fast, comfortable cars, the equal-wheel bogies under the HR2s giving a particularly smooth ride.

However, the LCC engineers under G.F. Sinclair, not to be out-manoeuvered by the competitors, built No 1 at Charlton works – it was the ultimate in London tramcar development. Painted royal blue it was soon dubbed *Bluebird* by the staff who presumably knew of *Bluebell* north of the Thames.

The new car, mounted on the bogies from HR2 No 160 and fitted with airbrakes, was designed to introduce a new era of luxury travel. Like the 'Feltham' the car was of composite construction with a steel underframe giving a one-floor level only 2ft 5in above rail level. The entrance doors and steps were air operated, and straight staircases gave easy access to the upper saloon where modern lighting was concealed in the coves of the white painted ceiling. The transverse seating was more generously spaced and well upholstered in blue moquette. Other refinements included opening louvre windows in the lower saloon, electric heaters, separate driver's cabs windscreen wipers and linoleum floor coverings.

No 1 was built for, and operated on, the subway services where the air operated front platform door could be used at the island platforms of the two subway stations at Aldwych and Holborn.

The most distinctive feature of the LCC trams was the destination display. On the newer cars large stencils, fore and aft and on the sides, displayed the service number (the LCC operated services, the route number being the running number of a car in a particular service), and a two or three line screen above the driver's head showed the tram's destination. On the E1s (except

London County Council Tramways No 1
Built: Charlton 1932
Length overall: – 36ft 0in
Width overall: 7ft 3in
Seats (lower saloon): – 28 TU 2+2
Seats (upper saloon): – 38 TU 2+2
Trucks: – EMB Equal wheel; 4ft 9in wheelbase 26½in diameter wheels
Motors: – 4 x MV 109; 35hp
Controllers: – MV
Brakes: – Hand wheel, air wheel, magnetic track

the rebuilt subway single-deck cars) the figures were composed of glass studs in a metal plate which was hung inside the top deck canopy and illuminated from behind. The glass studs of these 'Venner' numbers fell out or were removed in the course of time.

All cars carried sideboards at waist level; these gave detailed route information and extra boards advertised the '1/- all day' and '6d. Evening ticket'. No 1 had none of these and showed the route on blinds only.

There is no doubt that when the LCC system was transferred to the London Passenger Transport Board on 1 July 1933, it was at the height of its efficiency. The cars were fast and comfortable; fares were low and the tracks well maintained. Although 143 E1 cars were 'rehabilitated', a policy of replacement by trolleybus was inaugurated, and by 1940 trams were only operating in South London, Croydon and through the subway to Highgate and Manor House in the north.

The tramcar, however, still dominated the Thames Embankment and in the evening rush-hour a fast moving and continuous procession could be seen in both directions; E1s for Clapham Junction and Wimbledon, E3s for the subway, 'Felthams' for Streatham and Tooting, HR2s for Peckham Rye and Dulwich, and ex-East Ham or West Ham cars for Woolwich and Abbey Wood. Sadly No 1 made only the occasional sortie out of Telford Avenue depot on the 16X or 18X to Norbury.

The E1 was the classic LCC tramcar; it was fast and functional and its extra height, when compared with the replacing bus, gave a grandstand view of the passing scene, especially when passing the Kennington Oval during the cricket season. Inside it was white paint and notices, faretables on one bulkhead and a notice to keep the tram tidy on the other. The general chatter of the passengers and the ting of the Bell punch would be accompanied by a background noise of bogies on rail joints, the whine of the motors as the car accelerated away from a stop and the squeal of the magnetic brakes when it reached the next one.

The improved version, the 'E1' class, was built over a period of 20 years and included No 1423 of 1910 (*Above left*) seen without side destination boards south of Brockley Cross; No 1001, 'rehabilitated' in 1935 and only one of two without windscreens, at Stamford Hill (*Left*); and (*Below*) one of the 1727-1851 60hp series built by Hurst Nelson in 1921-22.
R. Wiseman/W. A. Camwell/Hurst Nelson, courtesy J. H. Price

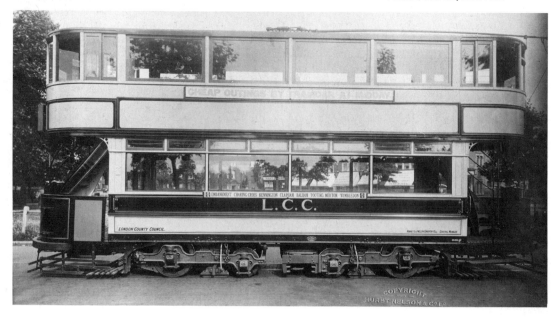

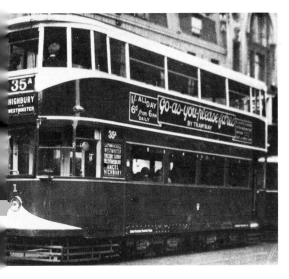

These delights were not to last. Replacement by diesel buses was completed on 5 July 1952 when E3 No 1951 arrived at New Cross depot well after midnight. Three HR2s, No 1 and most of the 'Felthams' saw further service in Leeds, and examples of these types are to be seen in museums.

Left:
No 1 in its original blue livery at Bloomsbury in 1933 – the LCC's final fling before being taken over by the LPTB.
M. J. O'Connor

Below:
The 'HR2' and 'E3' classes were the ultimate development of the 'E1'. 'HR2' class No 155 is in London Transport livery but with LCC style fleet numbers. The 101-160 batch were only equipped for conduit operation initially.
London Regional Transport

Birmingham

At the turn of the century Birmingham must have been a magnet to those with more than a passing interest in the transport scene. In addition to the many railway branch lines, there were horse, steam, cable and battery-powered tramcars operated by a number of local companies on tracks leased from the city and neighbouring local authorities.

The City of Birmingham Tramways Co Ltd was incorporated on 29 September 1896 to purchase and expand the tramways. This company opened the first overhead electric tramway, along the Bristol Road to Bournbrook, Selly Oak, on 13 May 1901. Under the wing of the British Electric Traction Co from 1902 onwards electrification and extension continued apace. The company overhaul works at Kyotts Lake Road, originally built for steam trams and trailers, also built a considerable number of tramcars between 1901 and 1905.

The Birmingham Corporation Act of 1903 empowered the Corporation to operate tramcars, and on 4 January 1904 the first Corporation car ran from Steelhouse Lane to Aston Brook Street. The initial batch of cars, Nos 1-20 from Preston, were destined to spend 40 years on the Perry Barr route; they were too high after top-covering to pass under the railway bridge at Aston station, and illustrate the longevity of the traditional tramcar in those areas where track and fleet maintenance were of a high order.

In essence narrow-gauge versions of the LCC 'D'

Birmingham Corporation Tramways Nos 1-20
Built: – Preston 1904
Length overall: – 31ft 6in
Length over corner posts: – 21ft 0in
Width overall: – 6ft 3in
Height to trolley plank: – 16ft 6in (1-10), 16ft 3in (11-20), when top-covered
Height inside lower saloon: – 6ft 9in
Height inside upper saloon: – 6ft 0in, when top covered
Stairs: – Reversed 180°, later normal 180°
Seats (lower saloon): – 27 LW; TU 2+1 1923-26
Seats (upper saloon): – 33 or 34 TW 2+1
Trucks: – Brill 22E; EMB 'Burnley' MaxT; 4ft wheelbase 1923-26 (Nos 4, 9, 10, 16 Brush 'Burnley')
Motors: – 2 x DK 25B 25hp or DK 6A 35hp; later DK 30B 40hp
Controllers: – DK C 1
Brakes: – Rheostatic; later Westinghouse magnetic, EMB track
Gauge: – 3ft 6in

class bogies, they originated as open-top four-window cars with reversed stairs, but were soon fitted with balcony top-covers. Nos 1-10 received the 'bow roof' type in June 1905 and the rest the flat type two years later. They were modernised during 1923-26 and fitted with normal

Below and above right:
Built at Preston in 1903 as open-top reversed stair bogie cars, Birmingham Nos 1-20 worked the Perry Barr route for 40 years or more. They were soon top-covered and then rebuilt and modernised in 1923-26: No 6 (*Above right***) with EMB 'Burnley' bogies was photographed at Perry Barr terminus.** *Tramway Museum Society/W. A. Camwell*

stairs, vestibuled platforms, upholstered 2+1 seats and chromium plated fittings in the lower saloon. The original Brill 22E bogies were replaced by EMB 'Burnley' bogies fitted with track brakes, except for Nos 4,9,10,16 which had spare sets of Brush 'Burnleys' ordered at that time. However, they retained their open balconies to the end and happy are the memories of sitting in the open front as we sped to town after the long, self-inflicted walk from Handsworth Wood to Perry Barr.

These original 20 cars were followed during the years up to 1913 by 430 'standard' Preston single-truck cars with three or four-window bodies. A large number of these cars were also renovated and re-equipped. Improvements included transverse seating inside, Numa air bells, 'Silvalux' light fittings and chromium plated rails and grab handles. The older electrical equipment was also replaced – for example DK 6A motors by BTH 248A, and C1 controllers by the K3 type.

The city boundaries were extended in 1911 and the Corporation took over the remaining company-operated services together with a motley selection of cars, including some built at Kyotts Lake Road, which now became the Corporation overhaul works. The 61 cars concerned, numbered 451-511, were re-equipped and fitted with new balcony top-covers except for 15 which were scrapped within a few years or converted to PW duties.

The only two bogie cars, Nos 451 and 452, had a long and eventful life. After operating as open-top cars they were converted to single-deck motor cars in 1917 for experiments with trailers. In 1926 they were extensively rebuilt and as five-window balcony cars on Mountain & Gibson 'Burnley' bogies they lasted to the closure of the Perry Barr route in 1949.

The Birmingham area tramways were built to the narrow 3ft 6in (1,067mm) gauge, and car capacity was a perennial problem, especially after 1920 when the expansion of the tramways on sleeper tracks to new housing estates and the take-over of the West Bromwich routes called for a fast, high-capacity fleet of trams.

Although experiments with single-deck trams and trailers had been made the Corporation decided to continue buying traditional bogie tramcars from the established firms, following the initial batches of open-balcony cars from UEC (Nos 512-586) in 1913-14 and from Brush (Nos 587-636) in 1920. These later had the balconies enclosed, transverse upholstered 2+1 seats in the lower saloon, and the majority upholstered seats upstairs as well. Many were also given new 63 or 70hp motors which made for fast running on the straight sections of line between Handsworth and West Bromwich.

These were followed by enclosed cars – Nos 637-661 from Midland Railway, Carriage & Wagon, in 1923, and Nos 662-731 and 732-761 from Brush during 1924-26. They all had four-window bodies and operated mainly from Miller Street and Selly Oak depots, serving the Aston and Bristol Road routes respectively.

Further new cars were bought in 1928 – Nos

Birmingham Corporation Tramways Nos 71-220
Built: Preston 1906-07
Length overall: – 28ft 8in
Length over corner posts: – 17ft 2in
Width overall: – 6ft 3in
Height to trolley plank: – 16ft 0½in
Height inside lower saloon: – 6ft 7in
Height inside upper saloon: – 6ft 0in
Stairs: – Direct 180°
Seats (lower saloon): – 24 LW; later TU 2+1
Seats (upper saloon): – 28TW 2+1
Trucks: – M&G Radial; later P35
Motors: – DK 6A 35hp; later GE 249A
Controllers: – DK G 1; later K 3
Brakes: – Westinghouse magnetic
Gauge: – 3ft 6in

Birmingham Corporation Tramways 1914 Brush-built
Standard double-deck bogie car No 580. *E. Thornton*

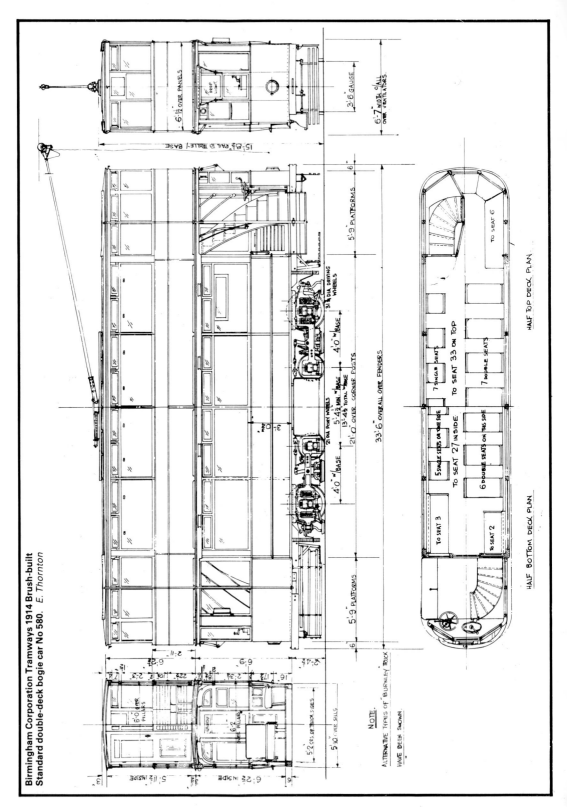

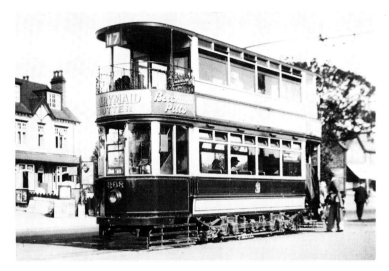

762-811 from Brush and Nos 812-841 from Short Bros of Rochester, which had been building bus bodies for Birmingham as well as the London General Omnibus Co. These new cars retained the standard four-window lower saloon with air scoops but the upper saloon had eight windows, 'each under the control of the person opposite to it', to quote the contemporary journals. They were equipped with air brakes and worked the Ward End and Pershore Road routes respectively, the former ones being fitted with bow collectors.

All these new cars, however, were of traditional designs, and although the later cars were faster and more comfortable their appearance was becoming dated by 1928. Their main drawback was weight, and at 16¾ tons power costs were high, especially at speed. To overcome this drawback two new lightweight cars, envisaged as prototypes for a new fleet, were built at this time, No 842 by Short Brothers in 1929 and No 843 by Brush a year later.

The bodies were of aluminium alloy (duralium) on underframes of steel for No 842, or steel and duralium for No 843. With lightweight motors and other equipments these cars achieved weight savings of three tons and four tons respectively, the former saving 17% on current consumption compared with the 1928-built trams on the Pershore Road.

In appearance No 843, retaining the eight window pattern to the upper saloon, was the more elegant vehicle, with rocker panels and a pronounced domed roof. No 842 had an uneven window pattern, a flatter roof and flush side panels.

The interior decor was orthodox, with bulkheads, veneered ceilings and unshaded lights, but the lower saloon had ventilation through the cove panels, into which the side destination screens were recessed. Ashanco air extractors were fitted in the roof. Ventilation was not really adequate under crush conditions on No 842 and additional ventilation was soon provided.

Birmingham Corporation Tramways

	Nos 587-636 Loughborough 1920	No 842 Rochester 1928	No 843 Loughborough 1930
Built:			
Length overall: –	33ft 6in	33ft 6in	33ft 6in
Length over corner posts: –	21ft 0in	21ft 0in	21ft 0in
Width overall: –	6ft 3in	6ft 3in	6ft 3in
Height to trolley plank: –	15ft 6in	15ft 6in	15ft 3¾in
Height inside lower saloon: –	6ft 2¾in	6ft 2⅞in	6ft 2¼in
Height inside upper saloon: –	6ft 0in	5ft 10⅛in	5ft 10¼in
Stairs: –	Direct 180°	Direct 90°	Direct 90°
Seats (lower saloon): –	28 LW; later TU 2+1	27 TU 2+1 brown moquette	27 TU 2+1
Seats (upper saloon): –	34 TW 2+1; later TU	36 TU 2+1 brown leather	33 TU 2+1
Trucks: –	Brush 'Burnley'; 4ft wheelbase	EE 'Burnley'; 26in/20in diameter wheels	EE 'Burnley' 26in/20in diameter wheels
Motors: –	2 x BTH GE 247A; 35hp	2 x EE DK105/3KP; 40hp	2 x GEC WT 28 AS; 40hp
Controllers: –	DK DB 1-K3B; later K33E	EE L33E + field shunt	GEC KA/1
Brakes: –	Magnetic, EMB Maley electro-mechanical	M&T airwheel and airtrack	
Gauge: –	3ft 6in	3ft 6in	3ft 6in

Birmingham lightweight cars

The lower saloon of No 842 illustrates the use of new materials in tramcar construction although the exposed light bulbs hardly help the modern image.
Tramway Museum Society

Like LCC No 1 these cars were the last of the line; although built of lightweight materials they were traditional in many ways and the cars may be termed transitional in design rather than classic. Be that as it may the body of car No 842 stood up to the rough and tumble of everyday use better than the lighter, newer car.

Birmingham's classic tramcars were the original open-balcony cars of 1904, the Preston single-truck cars and the enclosed bogies which dominated the Lichfield, Soho and Bristol Roads.

All the bogie cars had maximum traction bogies of the 'Burnley' type in which the guiding axle was held down on the track by a coil spring in compression. It was developed by Mr H.A. Mozley, the Burnley Corporation Tramways manager. These trucks gave good riding qualities and maximum adhesion, an important consideration on sleeper tracks at speed. Essentially standard products of Preston and Loughborough, the cars acquired a distinctive Birmingham look, both inside and out, through progressive improvements over the years, although polished woods remained the dominant feature. The Birmingham gauge gave the

trams a tall, narrow look, which was enhanced by the dark blue and primrose livery, the route number box at roof level and the absence of a destination screen in the upper deck panels. This latter feature gave good scope for advertisements, of which 'Evening Dispatch' was peculiar to the city. Two distinctive features were the extendable sunblind above the driver's windscreen and the aluminium cowl to the left protecting the handbrake handle.

As already indicated there was variety in the side window arrangements; the lower saloon had the traditional air scoops and hinged ventilators while upstairs there were half-drop sash windows, although narrow pivoted ventilators were a feature of the newer cars.

As can be seen from the illustrations destination information was minimal; the screens remained set throughout the day's journeyings and only needed changing to 'Depot Only' for the final run. On route 36 even this was not necessary as the depot was at the Cotteridge terminus and it is possible that the screens of Nos 842 and 843 remained unchanged for weeks at a time.

In some ways reminiscent of *Bluebell*, with its domed roof and eight saloon windows, No 843 is about to turn into Kyotts Lake Road.
Tramway Museum Society

Manchester

The Manchester Corporation Tramways ranked third in the British Isles, after London and Glasgow, with a maximum of 947 cars operating over 123 miles of route. They formed the centre of a large inter-urban network with Manchester cars penetrating outwards to Oldham and Waterhead (nine miles) in the east, to Hyde, Stockport and Hazel Grove (11 miles) in the southeast and to Rochdale (11 miles) in the northwest. Tramcars in the livery of Salford, South Lancashire, Rochdale, Oldham, Ashton, Stockport, Stalybridge Joint Board and Bury were to be seen in the centre of Manchester.

The Corporation had taken over the horse tramways of the Manchester Carriage & Tramways Co in stages between 1901 and 1903 and the first Corporation electric car ran on 6 June 1901. Two years previously six sample cars had been ordered from the various manufacturers for evaluation and the outcome was large orders for Brush and G.F. Milnes. Later cars were built mainly by UEC/English Electric and, from 1909 onwards, also in the Corporation's own works at Hyde Road.

The open-top short-canopy design, both bogie and single-truck, dominated until 1906, by which time over 600 had been delivered. There then followed 100 open canopy cars, and with 50 single-deck combination cars the fleet stood at 792 by the end of 1914. The majority of the open-top cars had been rebuilt or converted to the top-covered open balcony type by 1924, and more new enclosed bogie cars brought the fleet to its maximum during 1928.

The single-deck combination cars totalled 67 and included five purchased second-hand from the Middleton Electric Traction Co. They were used on the 53 route which followed a circuitous course round the Victorian suburbs of the city from Cheetham Hill in the northwest to Stretford in the west. Two low bridges prevented the use of double-deck cars on this service and it became the first casualty with buses taking over during 1930.

Traditional bogie cars of a more advanced design continued to be built as replacements for older cars until 1930 when a new 'Pullman' single-truck car appeared. To the specification of the new manager, Mr R. Stuart Pilcher, recently appointed from Edinburgh, the cars became known unofficially as 'Pilchers', and the last appeared in 1932.

Tramway abandonment now proceeded with increasing momentum and the fleet was down to around 370 cars when I first visited the city in July 1945. By this time all the open-canopy single-truck cars and many of the older bogie cars had been scrapped, and most services were operated with the newer enclosed double-deck bogie cars, which although mechanically sound were generally in a shabby condition. The single-truck 'Pilcher' cars were mostly housed at Hyde Road depot and were to be seen on the services to Oldham, Hyde and Fallowfield.

During the following years the number of cars in service declined, and after the sale of the 'Pilcher' cars during 1947-48, the dwindling number of bogie cars operated out of Birchfields Road depot. Finally, on 10 January 1949, the last car, No 1007, ran to West Point and then to Hyde Road, where, in

Manchester Corporation Tramways No 1007

Built: – Preston 1927
Length overall: – 35ft 0in
Length over corner posts: – 21ft 10½in
Length of platforms: – 6ft 0in
Width overall: – 7ft 3in
Height to trolley plank: – 16ft 6in
Stairs: – Direct 180°
Seats (lower saloon): – 32 TW 2+1;
later 28 TU 2+1
Seats (upper saloon): – 48 TW 2+2
Trucks: – Manchester MaxT (modified 22E type)
Motors: – 2 x BTH 509C; 50hp
Controllers: – BTH B510
Brakes: – Hand wheel, rheostatic

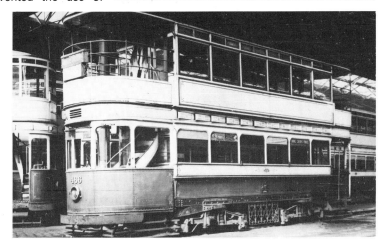

Brush and Milnes had built over 500 tramcars for Manchester by 1905.

The Brush series of open-top bogie cars, Nos 437-486, were built in 1901 and most, including No 466 shown here, were later fitted with balcony top covers. Brill 22E bogies replaced the original Brush B type.
W. A. Camwell

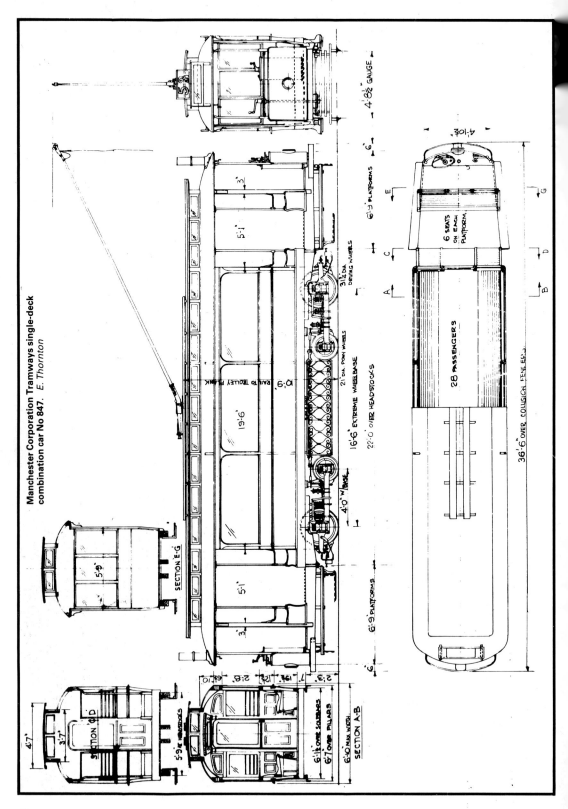

Manchester Corporation Tramways single-deck combination car No 847. *E. Thornton*

4·8½″ GAUGE

6′ 9″ PLATFORMS

3′

5′ 1″

RAILED TROLLEY PLANK

19′ 6″

10′ 9″

3′

3½″ DIA. DRIVING WHEELS

21″ DIA. PONY WHEELS

4′·0″ W. BASE

16′·6″ EXTREME WHEELBASE

22′·0″ OVER HEADSTOCKS

6′ 9″ PLATFORMS

5′ 1″

3′

6′

SECTION E-G

5′ 9″

SECTION C-D

4′·7″

3′·7″

5′·9″ HEADSTOCKS

6′·1½″ OVER SOLEBARS

6′·7″ OVER PILLARS

6′·0″ MAX. WIDTH

2′·3″ 7″ 19½″ 1½″ 2′·8″ 6′·10″

SECTION A-B

4·10½″

6 SEATS ON EACH PLATFORM

28 PASSENGERS

36′·6″ OVER COLLISION FENDER

E

C

A

G

D

B

the permanent way yard alongside the railway embankment, these bogie cars became the last of nearly a thousand trams – including some from Oldham, Ashton and Salford – to be burnt there over the years.

It will be seen from the above that Manchester had three types of classic tramcar; the single-deck combination, the 'standard' bogie and the 'Pilcher'.

The first 25 combination cars were built in 1903 by G.F. Milnes to a design registered by The Laconia Car Co of the USA and dating back to the late 1890s. Its main feature was a bench seat on the driving platforms, and as the Board of Trade objected to this arrangement on tramcars operating in urban areas, they were rebuilt with a narrow driving platform without passenger accommodation. Further batches of cars to this modified design were built by UEC and delivered in 1907 (20 cars), 1914 (five cars) and 1920-21 (12 cars). A further 10 cars purchased from the Middleton Electric Traction Co Ltd (BET) in 1925 were built by Brush in 1901, but only five were actually used by Manchester.

The main characteristics of the Manchester type were the three large saloon windows, the narrow driving platforms and the clerestory roof. Between the closed saloon, entered by sliding doors, and the platform bulkheads were open passenger areas. These areas had a bench seat facing inwards and two single seats over the sandboxes by the saloon bulkheads. Chains were fixed between the bulkheads to prevent passengers falling into the road.

The clerestory roof with its half lights of red glass extended to the full length of the passenger accommodation. The interior was all polished wood, with longitudinal seating and veneered ceiling.

Lighter than the Manchester bogie double-deck car, but fitted with the same 40hp motors, they could accelerate rapidly and show a good turn of speed, essentials on a route serving a heavily populated area.

After the abandonment of the 53 route most of these cars were scrapped. Last to survive was No 847 which remained until 1948 when it too made its way to the permanent way yard at Hyde Road. Fortunately enthusiasts were able to locate a number of 'combination' type bodies in various stages of decay, and eventually No 765, the best of these, was rescued from the moorlands above Huddersfield and painstakingly rebuilt; now fully restored it operates on the Heaton Park tramway.

Undoubtedly the classic tramcar in the Manchester area was the large enclosed bogie vehicle of traditional appearance, and although Salford had a fleet with many variations, the Manchester bogie car had a distinctive Mancunian look, and certainly by the time I knew them that look was a worn and untidy one, the faded red cream paint only shining when it rained, although

Few combination cars survived the demise of the 53 circular route in 1930. The last, No 847, shown outside Birchfields Road depot, met its fate in Hyde Road yard in 1948.
D. Conrad

one Saturday afternoon I saw a repainted dash reflecting brightly in the wet cobblestones of the Stockport Road.

The older cars with monitor ceiling were in a minority by 1945 so I was only familiar with those cars built after 1920 at Preston, Loughborough or at the Hyde Road works. They must have been elegant cars in their day – an elegance based on the civic pride of the Edwardian era and reflected in the fancy glass lampshades and the City Arms etched on the glass of the bulkhead doors.

The other classic features were the red glass ventilators, like those in London controlled by a handle in the middle, the light switches on the nearside bulkhead, the ventilators above the bulkhead doors, and the slightly curved and varnished patterned maple ceiling. The wooden longitudinal seats had, in most cases, been replaced by upholstered 2+1 transverse seats in dark blue leather cloth or green moquette. A few had transverse wooden seats, however.

The upper saloon appeared more spacious; it was slightly wider, but the 2+2 wooden seating was cramped and the gangway narrow. There were no bulkheads, a modern feature, and the stairwell could be covered by a stairtrap working on the jacknife principle when not in use. The window arrangement matched the lower saloon with opening quarter lights, but the main windows would let down into the sides and ventilation was no problem!

Although only 38 of the scheduled 40 new cars were built, the 'Pullman' or 'Pilcher' tram became a classic within its own lifetime probably because it

Manchester Corporation Tramways No 765
Built: – Preston 1913
Length overall: – 36ft 6in
Length over corner posts: – 19ft 6in
Width overall: – 6ft 8½in
Width over corner posts: – 6ft 6in
Height to trolley plank: – 10ft 6in
Height inside saloon: – 7ft 5in
Seats (saloon): – 28 LW laths; outside 12 TW
Trucks: – Brill 22E bogies
Motors: – 2 x Westinghouse 220; 30hp
Controllers: – DK DB1 K4
Brakes: – Hand wheel

was used as an excuse to abandon the tramway system. According to the press reports of the time these new cars, though fast, were unable to compete with the new buses then coming into service. Whatever the truth of the arguments the last of these cars was not scrapped until 1956 (in Aberdeen) to give an average lifespan of over 20 years.

They first appeared in February 1930; although very different to the standard bogie vehicle, they also had many similarities and retained the Mancunian look. The similarities arose because,

The Edwardian elegance of the Manchester tramcar is seen here in the internal monitor ceiling, the ruby ventilating lights and the fancy lampshades. The coat of arms etched in the glass of the door contrasts with the switches on the right-hand bulkhead.
Tramway & Railway World, courtesy J. H. Price

**Manchester Corporation Tramways 1920-class standard
double-deck bogie car.** *E. Thornton*

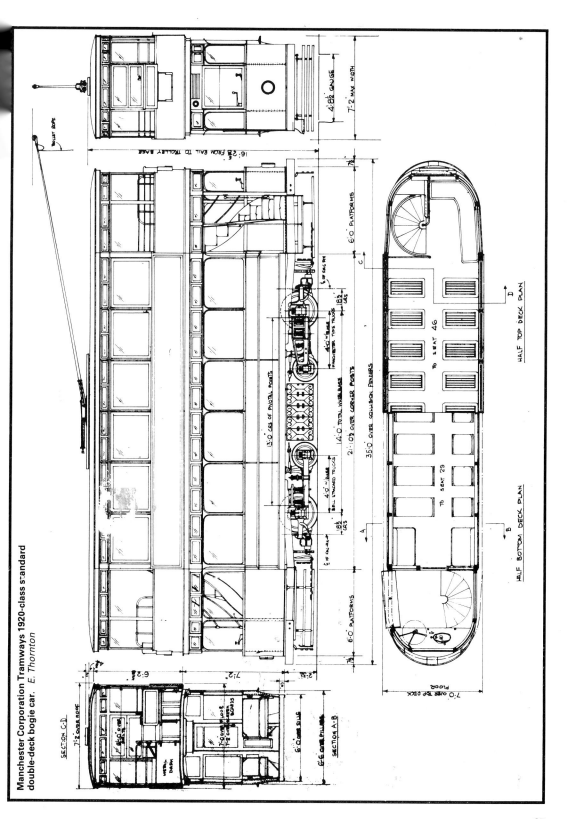

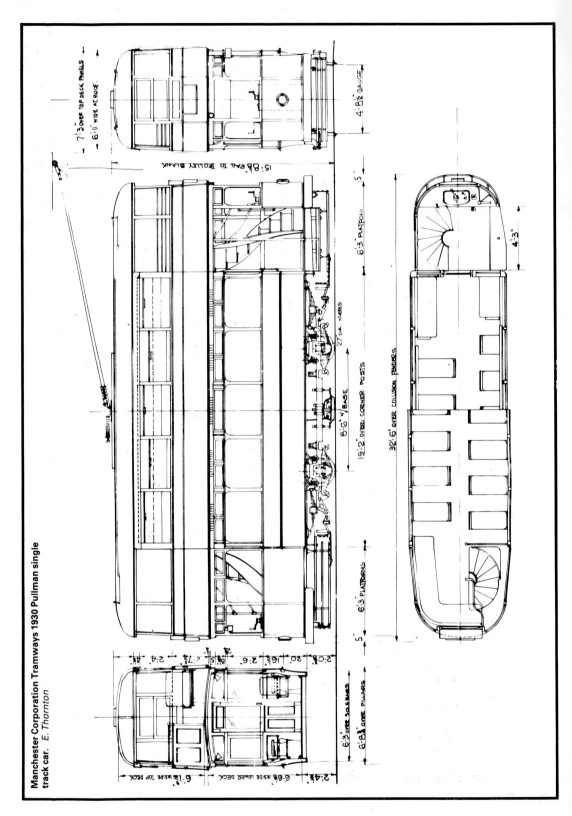

**Manchester Corporation Tramways 1930 Pullman single
track car.** *E. Thornton*

like all of Manchester's trams, the bodies were built largely of wood and Hyde Road used as many standard parts as possible. This was particularly so in the lower saloon windows, driver's vestibules and destination equipment – metal stencil plates for the service number fitting below the single destination screen. The rocker panel was retained, as were half turn staircase and quarter lights in the lower saloon.

The differences were to be seen in the modern low-slung body with domed roof; based on a Hurst Nelson underframe with downswept headstocks this allowed a lower saloon floor on the same level as the platforms. The upper saloon also had a modern look with sloping sides and ends, half-drop windows and upholstered seating.

The 'Pilchers' were fitted with 8ft wheelbase Peckham Pendulum P35 trucks, made by Brush under licence, and with two motors giving 100hp the cars could run up to speeds of 40mph or more. Certainly on one occasion we were pacing the express bus(!), from Nottingham, down the Stockport Road; an early morning run to Hollinwood, shortly before abandonment, when the car had all the power supply to itself, was exhilarating. At speed, with the pendulum gear easing the irregularities in the track, the riding was smooth enough, but the combination of an 8ft wheelbase and soft springing resulted in 'tailwag', and a bouncing, swinging motion, especially on worn track, could be alarming at times.

Manchester Exchange in 1947. Replacement bogie No 294 is at the head of the queue – note that the side destination box is now disused.

However, the design features were basically sound and the cars performed well with a high pitched whine and an oscillating motion. The soundness of the design could be seen when they moved to their new homes where years of neglect had first to be made good as only minimum maintenance, consistent with safety, had been carried out since November 1946.

During a visit to Leeds on a dull afternoon in November 1947 I was watching the procession of tramcars returning from the football ground at Elland Road when a grey domed-roof car appeared among them. It was obviously not one of the wartime purchases from Kingston-upon-Hull, but when it passed, its original home was given away by its shape and curly gold numerals above the headlamp, 287, last seen months previously. By a coincidence no Leeds car at that time was numbered 287. All these cars found new homes; seven went to Leeds, six to Sunderland, 11 to Edinburgh and 14 to Aberdeen.

At the end it was right that the last trams to run were the classic bogie cars, for over 600 were constructed; the first 285 with their elaborate monitor ceilings in the lower saloon were built by Brush in batches up to 1912 while the remainder of

Manchester Corporation Tramways No 287
Built: – Manchester 1931
Length overall: – 32ft 6in
Length over corner posts: – 19ft 2in
Length of platforms: – 6ft 3in
Width overall: – 7ft 3in
Width over corner posts: – 6ft 8¾in
Height to trolley plank: – 15ft 8⅛in
Height inside lower saloon: – 6ft 6⅛in
Height inside upper saloon: – 6ft 9 ¹⁄₁₆in
Stairs: – Direct 180°
Seats (lower saloon): – 22 TU 2+1 leather
Seats (upper saloon): – 40 TU 2+2 leather
Trucks: – Peckham P35; 8ft 6in wheelbase; 27in diameter wheels
Motors: 2 x MV 105; 50hp
Controllers: – BTH B510
Brakes: – Hand wheel, magnetic track

At speed they would roll along majestically with the gentle swaying motion characteristic of all bogie cars, and the wheels would beat a regular rhythm on the rail joints. Upstairs the swaying motion was more pronounced and reminds me of my only ride on route 32 through the streets of Gorton on 21 June 1945. This section was one of the few with single track with passing loops and the car was lightly loaded and the driver was in a hurry. Travelling at some speed the car would hit the points with a shattering blow, swing left and then right again as the bogies took the curve into the loop. Each time all the windows rattled in their frames, the characteristic of the Manchester trams, and I felt the two decks would come apart. However, the tram had been built soundly in the traditional manner and was to run for some years to come.

Sadly the classic Manchester tram with all its dignity was allowed to decay and I only remember it in its shabby neglected form; the new Manchester tram or railcar will be single-deck and very different from its ancestor. Meanwhile combination car No 765 is to be seen restored and resplendent carrying passengers again in Heaton Park.

more modern design had flat ceilings as described above.

They are best remembered in the half light of the evening rush hour when they would proceed in convoy along the Stockport Road towards Levenshulme; inside all the seats would be occupied and other passengers would be standing and holding the hanging straps tightly as the car accelerated away from Piccadilly or Ardwick Green. There would be a low pitched and increasing whine from the motors and a crescendo of sound with the whole car shuddering as each bogie hit the points, crossings or dipped joints.

Manchester 'Pullman' No 131 at Exchange terminus. Its destination is Hyde Market Place, 10 miles away.
M. J. O'Connor

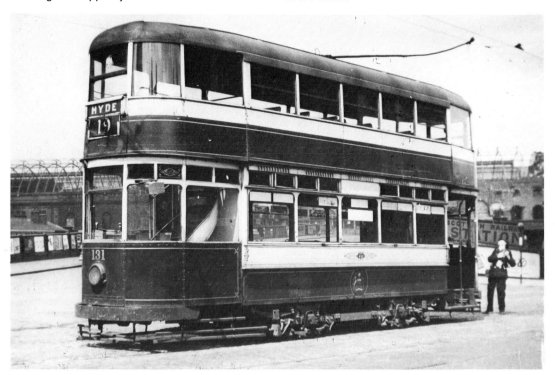

Liverpool

As we have seen in an earlier chapter Liverpool had amassed a total of over 300 standard open-top reversed-stair three-window 'Preston' cars by the end of 1901. These were followed by 30 more, the first five open-top, the others fitted with 'Bellamy' top covers.

The Corporation had taken over the Lambeth Road Carriage works from the Liverpool United Tramways & Omnibus Co on 1 September 1897 and had built the first electric trams there in 1899. During the early years of the century the works was busy building 'Bellamy' top covers for the open-top cars, but 110 new cars to the 'Preston' pattern were also turned out. The last appeared in 1913 by which time there were 446 'Prestons', essentially alike, out of a total fleet of 576 cars. This was an impressive degree of standardisation for a municipal fleet at that time.

The last series of cars had balcony top covers and more modern motors and equipment, but the oddest car, built at Preston at this time, was the prototype double staircase car, No 571. Lambeth Road built a further 26 to slightly modified designs in the next few years, but an experimental bogie car with centre entrance, also built at Preston, remained a one-off job even though it was Liverpool's first enclosed top-deck car and in many ways ahead of its time. These cars were designed for rapid loading and unloading on busy routes and incorporated a system of passenger flow.

Liverpool Corporation Tramways Nos 142-441
Built: – Preston 1900-02
Length overall: – 27ft 6in
Length over corner posts: – 16ft 0in
Length of platforms: – 5ft 0in
Width overall: – 7ft 6in
Width over corner posts: – 6ft 9in
Height to trolley plank: – 16ft 6in
Height inside lower saloon: – 6ft 6in
Height inside upper saloon: – 6ft 3in (when top covered)
Stairs: – Reversed 90°
Seats (lower saloon): – 22 LW
Seats (upper saloon): – 42 TW 2+2
Trucks: – Brill 21E; 6ft wheelbase 27in diameter wheels
Motors: – 2 x Walker 33S; 25hp*
Controllers: – Walker S1*
Brakes: – Hand wheel and rheostatic

* Imported from the USA until production started at Preston in about March 1900. The Walker 33S motor became the Dick Kerr No 25 type A and the S1 controller the DB1 Form A.

To meet the severe shortage of rolling stock after the war 30 reversed stair balcony cars were ordered from English Electric, Preston in 1919. This was a stop-gap measure and by the following year Lambeth Road was back in full production, and after 34 new or rebuilt open balcony cars with direct stairs, the works completed a further 321 cars

No 451, photographed at Clayton Square on 21 April 1950 in its final form on an EMB flexible axle truck, was one of the last 'Priestly' cars to be built.

Liverpool Corporation Tramways Nos 770-776
Built: – Liverpool 1933
Length overall: – 34ft 0in
Length over corner posts: – 21ft 0in
Length of platforms: – 6ft 6in
Width overall: – 7ft 4in
Width over corner posts: – 6ft 11½in
Height to trolley plank: – 15ft 5⅞in
Height inside lower saloon: – 6ft 5⅜in
Height inside upper saloon: – 5ft 10⅞in
Stairs: – Direct 90°
Seats (lower saloon): – 28 TU 2+2 Rexine
Seats (upper saloon): – 38 TU 2+2 Rexine
Trucks: – EMB Equal wheel heavyweight; 4ft 9in wheelbase; 26¼in diameter wheels
Motors: – 4 x CP; 36hp
Controllers: – CP
Brakes: – EMB air-wheel, rheostatic, magnetic track, electric runback

with enclosed balconies. These also had direct stairs and the last were built as late as 1933 in the new Edge Lane works, by which time they had evolved into an all-enclosed low-loading car with a wide body and transverse upholstered seating.

The 'Priestly' standard cars of 1922 had side windows which did not match; the four-window upper saloon above an almost pure 'Preston' three-window lower saloon gave the car an odd look. There were no bulkheads in the enclosed top deck and so for safety a trap door had to be fitted at the top of each staircase. This had a folding 'Priestly' seat which became available for use when the trapdoor was lowered at the driver's end. These cars were also fitted with automatic electric runback brakes.

No 757, an experimental 'luxury' single-deck bogie car, was built in 1929 by English Electric, and this car, together with double-deck bogie cars Nos 758-769, brought the fleet total to 769 at the start of the new era in 1933.

Like the tides on the Mersey, the tramways had reached a low ebb by 1932 with about two-thirds of ths fleet over 25 years old and most cars of obsolete design. At this time, however, the tide turned and it was decided to extend and modernise the tramways, and for this purpose a large number of new cars would be required for operation on the reserved tracks, existing and projected.

Nos 758-769 of 1931 were extended versions of the 'Priestly' cars with four-window saloons and five-window top decks; in both designs the lower saloon pillars had the necessary strength to support the weight above.

The first new car created a sensation; the standard Liverpool livery had been crimson lake and cream, but No 770 of 1933 appeared in a new green livery with a white stream-like effect, similar to that applied to LCC No 1, and was soon dubbed the 'Green Goddess' after a popular melodrama of the time. These cars had a teak frame with mahogany panels but retained the window arrangement of the previous series. Half-turn stairs were fitted and the upper saloon was entered by a swing door in the stairhead vestibule. The lower saloon was entered by double sliding doors and in both the white painted ceilings and concealed lighting gave an air of spaciousness.

The cars, with their floor level only 2ft 5⅞in above rail level, were mounted on the new heavyweight EMB 'radial arm' bogies with Hoffman bearings, which had been successfully demonstrated under the new LCC HR2 cars. The air-wheel service braking was controlled by a simple lever on the controller top, and with four motors these cars heralded the new era.

The first eight of these had flat roofs, but the elliptical roof was introduced with No 777 and this design formed the basis for the domed-roof cars which followed. Known as the 'Cabins' and the

The original 'Green Goddess' of 1933 retained the uneven windows of the 'Priestley' standard car but the ventilating lights had disappeared. No 775 was on Great Crosshall Street on 2 September 1952.

Liverpool streamliners

'Marks Bogies', they were in many ways the most elegant cars to run in Liverpool; they combined modern equipments with traditional looks which were enhanced by the slight tapering to the domed roof.

The 'Cabin' cars, Nos 782-817, so called from the separate driver's cabin, were 2ft longer and had matching half-drop windows, four to each saloon. They also had platform doors and straight reversed stairs. The 'Marks Bogies', Nos 818-867, which followed in 1933, were similar in outline but with normal stairs and no platform doors. EMB heavyweight bogies were standard for the 'Cabin' cars, but some of the 'Marks Bogies' had the newer EMB lightweight type and one, No 819, ran on EE bogies.

The development of the Liverpool tramcar reached its zenith with the advent of the streamlined bogie car, produced at the rate of approximately three a week from late in 1936 to the end of 1937 at Edge Lane works. Based on a steel underframe the body was of composite construction with pillars and rails of oak, other rails of ash, and aluminium exterior panelling. The lower saloon floor was of pine covered with cork tiles and separated from the vestibules by draught screens of toughened glass.

The platforms had a wide entrance with manually controlled double folding doors and, after the first two treads which gave a 90° turn, a straight staircase to the upper saloon. This was fitted with two rows of double reversible seats upholstered in leather. Both saloons had aluminium ceilings, polished mahogany facias and the panels below window level covered with leather cloth.

In addition to half-drop windows, ventilators in the roof and in the lower saloon panels were also fitted. Specially designed lampshades which extended out from the roof curves gave an even illumination.

The cars were fitted with electro-pneumatic control equipment located under one staircase. The other was used to house the air compressor. This equipment enabled the driver, who had a portable seat, to use a small master controller in place of the heavy traditional type, while the new system of multi-notch control gave smooth acceleration and braking under all conditions. The controller had 22 power and brake notches with intermediate notches on either side of the 'off' position to control the air-wheel and air-track brakes.

These cars were designed for frequent stops and rapid acceleration in the older heavily populated parts of the city, and for fewer stops and faster running on the sleeper tracks then being extended into the new suburbs. Their high seating capacity was also valuable under these conditions when most people still depended on public transport.

A total of 175 cars were scheduled to be built, but in the event the last 12 were cancelled and their bogies used under Nos 758-769 or as spares. Numbered 868-992 and 151-188, the rest had EMB heavyweight or lightweight bogies except for Nos 918-942 which were on Maley & Taunton bogies.

The last new cars to be built were 100 'Baby Grands' numbered 201-300. The bodies were similar to the bogie streamliners and they had EMB

Liverpool Corporation Tramways Nos 151-188, 868-992
Built: – Liverpool 1936-37
Length overall: – 36ft 9in
Length over corner posts: – 22ft 0in
Length of platforms: – 4ft 9in (entrance doors)
Width overall: – 7ft 4in
Height to trolley plank: – 15ft 0in
Height inside lower saloon: – 6ft 1½in
Height inside upper saloon: – 5ft 11in
Stairs: – Straight, 90° turn at the bottom
Seats (lower saloon): – 34 TU 2+2 leather
Seats (upper saloon): – 44 TU 2+2 leather
Trucks: – EMB equal wheel heavyweight or lightweight; 4ft 9in wheelbase*
Motors: – 4 x GEC WT184A; 40hp
Controllers: – MV electro-pneumatic
Brakes: – MV Air wheel and track

* Nos 918-942 had Maley & Taunton bogies

Bogie No 917 as rebuilt with sliding window vents and solid collision fenders, here at the Byrom Street-Dale Street junction on 4 September 1955.

hornless trucks of 9ft wheelbase. They were built during 1938-39, with the last three entering service in 1942. In addition to all the new cars it should be noted that 73 of the older cars, mainly of the 'Priestly' type, were modernised and fitted with new EMB trucks.

The modernisation policy saw the Liverpool system expand and flourish to a maximum of 784 cars in 1939 of which 373, or nearly half, were of modern design.

When I first knew Liverpool the streamlined cars were in a poor state, the bodies had not stood up to intensive use and the cars had a drooping look. Although a decision to abandon the system had been taken in 1945, 146 of these cars were rebuilt at Edge Lane works during 1950-53. The rebuilding included new oak pillars, replacement of the half-drop windows by the sliding type and the fitting of solid metal collision fenders instead of the original stainless steel strip ones. They were painted in the new lighter green livery and were kept in good condition to the end. During 1953-54 following the abandonment of the Garston and Muirhead Avenue routes, 46 cars were sold to Glasgow, including No 869 (Glasgow 1055) now preserved at Crich.

The one feature that stood out at the front of the Liverpool tram was the route number and destination display which filled all the space between the driver's windscreen and the top-deck window. The screen positions varied and only with the streamlined cars was the position standardised. The need for full information was because of the alternative routes available to the Pier Head, normally via Dale Street or Church Street, and the many other alternative workings to and from the suburbs. Also at this time there was a trend to give as much route information as possible on public service vehicles; for example the new buses and trolleybuses then replacing Manchester trams also gave detailed information. It was almost as though one of the advantages of the bus over the tram was the former's ability to show maximum route detail.

Inside, green and white were the dominant colours on all except the oldest cars. The offside bulkhead or draught screen in the newer cars was used to display the fare tables, very necessary with transfers and workmen's returns available on the tramcars. The maximum fare of 4½d (2p) allowed a through journey from Kirkby to the Pier Head (over nine miles) with 5d fares on the cross city routes Gillmoss to Woolton or Dingle.

There is no doubt that the memorable feature of the Liverpool streamlined bogie cars was their speed. They could accelerate rapidly to the 30mph authorised by the Ministry of Transport on the enclosed tracks, and riding on newly laid track was superb. The 'Baby Grands', however, were too long for their trucks and often resembled the Isle of Man packet when travelling at speed.

Sheffield

The Sheffield Corporation Tramways was an efficient system with a high reputation within the industry. This reputation was based upon good track maintenance and a progressive policy of fleet renewal, with very few passenger cars living to a ripe old age.

Sheffield is surrounded by hilly country, especially to the west, and horse tramways were only built along the roads following the river valleys. The Corporation took control of these lines at midnight on 7 July 1896 and proceeded to electrify and expand the system. Nearly all the new lines included at least one steep hill and this fact, together with some sharp curves, was the main reason for the use of single-truck cars throughout the life of the tramways.

The first electric car ran on 5 September 1899, and during the next 60 years the evolution of the electric tramcar was to be demonstrated in the Sheffield streets. The earliest vehicles were short-canopy cars of classic design from G.F. Milnes, and five-window single-deck cars for those routes involving steep hills or low bridges. They totalled 172 and 69 cars respectively.

These were followed by traditional top-covered open balcony cars, and by 1914 a total of 343 vehicles were in service including the 15 'Preston' cars built in 1907, the only passenger cars destined to see more than 50 years in passenger service. Unusually these Preston-built cars had 'Tudor Arch' windows, the distinctive feature of all Sheffield double-deck cars up to that time.

Sheffield was one of the first cities to introduce airbrakes and as a result the Board of Trade allowed double-deck cars on those routes with steep hills; when the roadway under Upwell Street bridge was lowered during 1919-20 the single-deck cars became redundant. Some cars were converted to double-deckers, some were sold to other undertakings (including Preston), and a few were converted to snowploughs. One such car, No 46, became snowplough No 354 in 1920 and so survived to be preserved when the tramway operation ceased in October 1960. Unfortunately the conversion process involved the removal of the central window, but with seats ex-Milnes car No 133, which had survived as a cafe in the Peak District, ran in the final tram procession to Beauchief and back.

Although most of the fleet had been purchased from outside firms – G.F. Milnes, Brush, UEC and Cravens – a number had been built at the Corporation workshops, first at Nether Edge and later at Queens Road. Further additions were now needed and in 1918 a prototype car, No 366, was built at Queens Road. The new design was based on ideas going back to 1911 when plans were drawn up for conversion of the remaining open-top double-deck cars to covered top. Three drawings were produced showing four-window cars as:-

(a) then being converted with short end top covers;
(b) having extended canopy open balcony covers;
(c) completely enclosed.

'Preston' car No 259 (later No 337) had already been modified to pattern C (circa 1909) and was the city's first enclosed tramcar. As a result the new design as seen in No 366 of 1918 was a five-window enclosed car built on traditional lines. The works, however, was too busy with arrears of maintenance, and later with building new enclosed top-covers for the 1913-14 series of balcony cars, so that only three of the new cars, Nos 367-369, were built there. The remainder were by Brush (Nos 376-450 in 1919-21 and Nos 36-60 in 1924-25) and by Cravens (Nos 451-500 in 1926-27).

The new cars were known as the 'Rocker Panel' class, at least to enthusiasts, on account of their classic design. They were large wooden-framed cars, and those built prior to 1921 seated 76

The Sheffield 'Rocker Panel' cars

The design for these 150 cars could be traced back to 1911. No 471, built by Cravens of Sheffield in 1925, shows off the 'banjo glass' and P22 truck in Tinsley depot in April 1956.

Sheffield Corporation Tramways No 376
Built: – Loughborough 1919
Length overall: – 33ft 0in
Length over corner posts: – 20ft 6in
Length of platform: – 5ft 7in
Width over corner posts: – 7ft 0¾in
Height to trolley plank: – 15ft 7½in
Height inside lower saloon: – 6ft 5in
Height inside upper saloon: – 5ft 10⅝in
Stairs: – Direct 180°
Seats (lower saloon(; 28 LW
Seats (upper saloon): – 48 TW 2+2; later 37 TW 2+1
Trucks: – Peckham P22 Maley type; 8ft 6in wheelbase; 33in diameter wheels
Motors: – 2 x BTH GE 203; 40hp
Controllers: – BTH
Brakes: – Hand wheel, air wheel and track

Above left:
A new standard tram was introduced in 1926: it featured flush sides and upholstered seats on both decks. No 200 in the traditional dark blue and cream livery takes on passengers at Leopold Street Junction. *Mrs A. R. Wiseman*
Above:
The domed roof cars in the new livery of cream with azure blue bands were probably the most attractive vehicles ever seen in Sheffield. No 236 is at the top of Angel Street in April 1947.

passengers: longitudinal in the lower saloon and 2+2 transverse upstairs – all in wood. The upper-deck seating was clearly too cramped, the seats being too short and the gangway too narrow. This problem was overcome by replacing one row of double seats by singles. This brought seating capacity down to 65, but the remaining cars of this class always seated 68 of which 40 were on top.

The key to this large capacity was the long wheelbase single truck. The early trucks had been of 6ft wheelbase, but the new Peckham P22 type modified by Maley and extended to a wheel base of 8ft 6in became standard in Sheffield for all cars built between 1918 and 1939.

The most distinctive feature of the 'Rocker Panel' cars was the vestibule and canopy ends with their curved glasses. In addition, to accommodate the brake handle, there was a 'banjo glass' in the driver's vestibule, and for the same reason the dash had a narrow outward extension at the top. These features also allowed more room on the platforms. The interior was varnished light oak with three-ply birch veneer on the ceilings.

In 1926 an entirely new car was designed and the prototype, the second No 1, was built by Cravens; it was probably the last car built by the firm. It represented the start of the fleet renewal programme and by 1936 there were 210 cars to this design, Nos 1-35, 61-130, 156-220 and 243-248 built at Queens Road and Nos 131-155 built by Hills of South Shields. In these cars the underframes were of rolled steel section, the body framing of teak and the exterior panelling aluminium.

Officially known as the 'Standard 1926' class and in many ways similar to the 'Rocker Panels', the main improvements were flush sides and the plain dashes. They retained the five side windows, quarter lights and framed windows upstairs, but the seating was improved with transverse 2+1 upholstered seats on both decks. They were superseded by the 'Standard 1936' class which was built at Queens Road up to 1939 and totalled 67 cars numbered 231-242 and 249-303. To replace vehicles lost during the war a further 14 bodies to this design were built to bring the final total to 81, two replacing those of the same type.

This design completed the first phase of the transition from the traditional to the modern as reflected in the Sheffield fleet. The new car tapered upwards from the waist rail to a domed roof which extended round the vestibule ends. This removed the top-heavy look seen in earlier designs to produce one of the most attractive tramcars ever seen.

The method of construction was similar to the previous series, with steel under-frames, teak body framing and aluminium for the interior and ceiling panels in addition to the exterior panelling. Considerable efforts were made to reduce noise by the use of insulating materials in the floors and by rubber pads inserted between body and truck. The use of helical gears also assisted in this respect.

The interior was also improved; the ceiling panels on both decks curved down to the top window rail and housed the semi-concealed lighting units. In the lower saloon ventilation was through air extractors fitted in the panels above the outer side windows; the central one housed the

Sheffield Corporation Tramways, No 264
Built: – Sheffield 1937
Length overall: – 32ft 7in
Width overall: – 7ft 3in
Height to trolley plank: – 16ft 2½in (overall)
Height inside lower saloon: – 6ft 3in
Height inside upper saloon: – 6ft 0in
Stairs: – Direct 180°
Seats (lower saloon): – 24 TU 2+1 moquette
Seats (upper saloon): – 37 TU 2+1 moquette
Trucks: – Peckham P22 Maley type, 8ft 6in wheelbase; 33in diameter wheels
Motors: – 2 x MV 102 DR; 50hp
Controllers: – BTH B510
Brakes: – Hand wheel, M&T air wheel and track, magnetic emergency

destination screens. All windows were of the half-drop type except for the centre window in the lower saloon. These windows were individually operated and protected by louvres which extended for the full length of the saloon. They replaced the rack and pinion operated framed type of the earlier designs.

White painted ceilings, the improved lighting and the 'semi-bucket' seats of moquette-covered 'Dunlopillo' made these vehicles attractive to passengers. The use of lightweight materials in body construction, lightweight motors and other electrical equipment gave quiet operation and low running costs.

The final stage of tramcar development in Sheffield was based on 'Jubilee' car No 501, built at Queens Road in 1946 to commemorate 50 years of municipal transport in the city. The car designed in the Department's drawing office had four side windows, platform doors and new style vestibule ends with an increased upward taper. It became the prototype for the 35 'Jubilee' class cars built by Charles Roberts of Horbury, between 1950 and 1952, the last new double-deck single truck cars to be built in the world.

The new cars, unlike the prototype design, had an all-metal structure on an underframe of mild steel channels. The main pillars were of high tensile steel and the main rails of mild steel extended for the whole length of the body sides. The whole structure was reinforced by diagonal bracing and truss panels, and all main body panels were constructed on jigs and easily removed if damaged. Protective primers were applied to resist corrosion of the metal, and after 30 years, some 20 of these at Crich, the metal frame of No 510 is still sound.

All exterior panels were of aluminium and the floors tongue and grooved softwood covered with terra cotta-coloured linoleum. Ventilation in the lower saloon was by air extractors in the panels above the windows and in the upper saloon by roof ventilators. Sliding opening vents in chromium

plated frames were also provided in the upper part of each saloon window.

Although double folding doors enclosed the platforms, the traditional lower saloon bulkheads were retained and entrance to the saloon was through sliding doors. The staircases were of the standard Sheffield half-turn type but the entrance door to the upper saloon had been eliminated. This saloon had four glazed roof lights on each side.

Seating was of the usual high standard, green moquette in the lower saloon and red leather in the upper. The interior panels were lined with leather cloth to match the seating and all wood was polished mahogany.

These cars, which were popular with both passengers and staff, had a relatively short life in the city, but the two cars now operating at museum sites, No 510 at Crich and No 513 at Beamish, are a fitting memorial to the quality of comfort and service once provided by the tramcar in Sheffield.

The tramcar was dominant in the Sheffield transport scene until 1954 when the abandonment programme started in earnest, although the high standard of maintenance continued almost to the end. Only some of the earlier 'Rocker Panel' cars were drooping at the platforms or working loose in the joints by the time they were withdrawn, while some of the 1927 Standard cars had their lower saloons rebuilt to the 1936 design to produce a very pleasing vehicle.

The classic Sheffield tramcars were built to straightforward, practical designs and were always distinctive. The services operated were never allocated route numbers and the two single blind destination screens did not detract from simple front end designs. The many times varnished dark blue livery with its elaborate lining out and large shaded numerals was retained on the older cars, but a new livery in which cream was the dominant colour, similar to that of present day buses in Eastbourne, was applied to all cars built or rebuilt after 1935. Advertisements were not introduced until 1950, and then were only placed on the side panels.

Sheffield also retained the trolley pole for current collection and all termini and important intermediate reversing points were provided with automatic trolley reversers. Each car carried a bamboo pole for use in emergency.

The most distinctive interior feature was the nearside bulkhead mirror in the lower saloon. This feature was introduced in the 1927 Standard cars to give a feeling of extra spaciousness. Improved quality mirrors with a simple etched design and bevelled edges were standard on the newer designs of car. In these later cars also, the driver had a portable seat on a stick which could be slotted into the platform at either end.

The riding qualities of the cars were second to

none. However, on the Beauchief reservation the 1936 domed-roof cars tended to sway gently from side to side, while the 'Jubilee' or Roberts cars had a slight fore and aft motion brought about by the springing on the 9ft wheelbase trucks. Finally, as recorded by Peter Handford in February 1959, the sound of the late-night Sheffield tram would carry on the night air as it sped down Abbey Lane until the squeal of the wheels would announce that it had turned Beauchief corner and was heading back towards the city.

Rotherham lies six miles down the Don valley from Sheffield and the town's first electric tramcar ran on 31 January 1903 from the Rawmarsh Road depot to the pumping station on Dalton Road. On 8 June 1903 Rotherham trams reached the then Sheffield boundary at Tinsley, but the jointly operated through service to Sheffield did not commence until September 1905. The service continued until 10 December 1948 when the closure of Bawtry Road bridge for reconstruction severed the tram tracks.

By 1933 the rebuilt 'Preston' cars operating the service were in poor condition and modern replacements were ordered. The new cars, Nos 1-6, were delivered in 1934 and proved to be so popular that five more were ordered for delivery the following year. These cars were single ended and built specifically for the through service which had loop terminals at each end. Apart from Liverpool No 5, built as an experiment in 1901 and converted to double-ended in 1902, they were the only cars so built for service in the British Isles, although Plymouth Corporation modified a number of cars for use on circular services.

The cars were built by the English Electric Co at Preston, and the first six were fitted with some equipment from scrapped cars. The bodies were of

Rotherham Corporation Tramways Nos 1-12
Built: – Preston 1934-35
Length overall: – 30ft 1in over fenders; body length 29ft 3in
Width overall: – 7ft 1in
Height to trolley plank: – 15ft 11in
Height inside lower saloon: – 6ft 1in
Height inside upper saloon: – 5ft 10in
Stairs: – Straight
Seats (lower saloon): – 27 TU 2+2 moquette
Seats (upper saloon): – 36 TU 2+2 leather
Trucks: – EMB flexible axle; 8ft 6in wheelbase; 33in diameter wheels (Nos 7-11, 28in diameter wheels)
Motors: – 2 x GEC, 40hp ex-scrapped cars. Nos 7-11 GEC WT 294, 40hp
Controllers: – GEC TE5/RIZ at front; DK DB1 at rear; Nos 7-11 GEC KH7 both ends
Brakes: – EMB air wheel, air track, rheostatic and magnetic emergency

composite construction, and in looks the cars resembled the trolleybuses of the period with twin headlights, two part windscreens and full width cabs. The driver could enter from the lower saloon or by an offside door.

The platform at the rear end was fitted with hinged doors with an emergency door on the offside. The one straight staircase was also on the offside and all seats faced forward. The saloons had half-drop windows, and thermostatically controlled heaters were fitted.

The trucks were of the EMB flexible axle type as used in Sunderland, and in addition to the driver's controller at the front, another was provided for emergency use on the rear platform.

The cars, in a pleasing blue and white livery, operated the through service to Sheffield until its closure on 11 December 1948, and the Templeborough short workings until this too was closed on 13 November 1949.

Jubilee car No 501 was the prototype for the 'Roberts' car of 1950. The last of the line, No 536, is seen at Holme Lane junction in 1954.

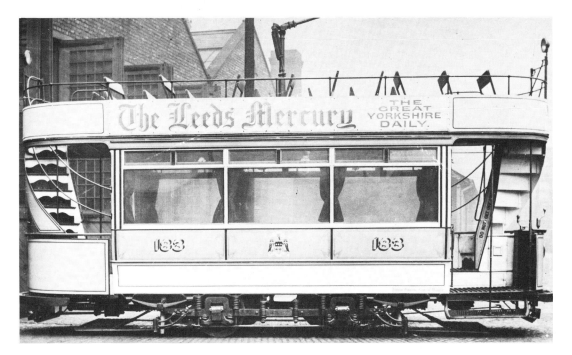

Standard 'Preston' reversed-stair cars were the backbone of the Leeds system for many years. No 183, the first of an order for 100 cars, was delivered in 1901. *Courtesy R. Brook*

Leeds

In tramway history Leeds has two claims to fame. On 11 November 1891 the first electric tram in Europe to use overhead current collection ran to Roundhay Park, and on 2 August 1897 Leeds became the second municipality to open an electric tramway system.

Development was then rapid and by 1905 over 280 cars were operating in the city and suburbs. The earliest were of the short canopy type, but by now there were also 175 'Preston' three-window open-top extended canopy cars with reversed stairs, which were top covered in due course. Further traditional cars added to the fleet were Hurst Nelson four-window open balcony cars (Nos 280-369) and the enclosed cars, later known as the 'Beeston air brakes', built at the Kirkstall Road works during 1923-24, (Nos 370-392, 402 and 399).

By this time the need to replace the older stock had become urgent and the result was 200 new enclosed cars over the next three years – Nos 1-75 from Brush, Nos 76-150 from English Electric and 50 built at Kirkstall Road (Nos 393-398, 400 and 403-410 with old bodies and 411-445 with new).

The new cars, seating 72 passengers (26+46) were longer than the earlier cars, and became notorious for their pivotal trucks supplied by EMB. The design of these trucks was based on the radial principle and was an attempt to make a 10ft wheelbase two-axle truck operate like two bogies, but the pivoting mechanism was soon locked solid and the now rigid trucks increased track wear, especially on curves.

Mr R.L. Horsfield, who had developed the lowbridge car in Cardiff, came to Leeds in 1928 and introduced a very successful type of tramcar. The prototypes, Nos 151-154, were built at Kirkstall Road, while the 100 production cars came from Loughborough during 1931.

These straight-sided cars had a main frame of Burma teak, a rolled steel underframe and the body was strengthened by truss plates. The exterior panels of the lower saloon were of sheet aluminium and those of the upper saloon African mahogany. The interiors had birch side panels, oak end panels and Burma teak for the interior finishes. The ceiling veneers were white enamelled and divided into sections by polished teak mouldings.

Although these cars had pivoted ruby light ventilators in the lower saloon and the upper saloon drop windows were controlled by a ratchet system, they had a solid, pleasing look which was enhanced by the raised dash panels screening the controller and brake handles. Platform doors were fitted at a later date. They had very efficient brakes, rode well on both street and sleeper track, and as the only cars able to run on all routes in normal

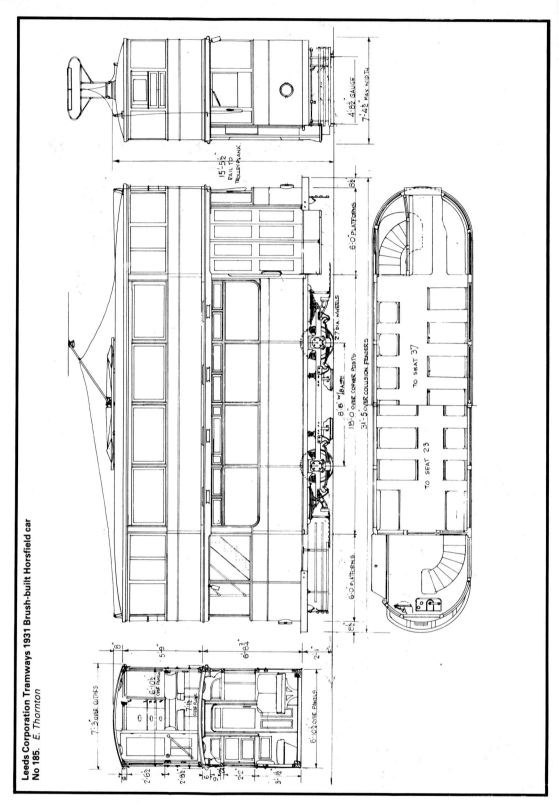

**Leeds Corporation Tramways 1931 Brush-built Horsfield car
No 185.** *E. Thornton*

Leeds City Transport Nos 155-254
Built: – Loughborough 1931
Length overall: – 31ft 5in
Length over corner posts: – 18ft 0in
Length of platform: – 6ft 0in
Width overall: – 7ft 4½in
Height to trolley plank: – 15ft 5½in
Stairs: – Direct 90°
Seats (lower saloon): – 23 TU 2+1 red hide
Seats (upper saloon): – 37 TU 2+1 red hide
Trucks: – Peckham P35; 27in diameter wheels
Motors: – 2 x BTH509; 60hp; 2 x GEC WT 28, 60hp cars
205-254
Controllers: – BTH B 525C; GEC KA 1A cars 205-254
Brakes: – Hand wheel and track, air wheel and track,
rheostatic and magnetic track

service, served Leeds until the end of tramway operation on 7 November 1959; a fitting tribute to the soundness of their design and traditional methods of construction.

Another classic tramcar was the Middleton Bogie, the brainchild of Mr Vane Morland who became manager in 1932. The type was designed specifically to work on the Middleton Light Railway which incorporated over 3½ miles of segregated tracks on which a maximum speed of 30mph was later allowed. No 255, the Brush-built prototype car, entered service in 1933 and was so successful that a further 16 were delivered in 1936 and took over the Middleton service for the next 20 years or more.

The body was of composite construction with the usual teak framing and ash roof sticks. The cars featured separate drivers cabs, manually operated double folding doors and straight staircases. The prototype car had offside staircases, but as this caused platform congestion the production cars, Nos 256-263 from Brush and Nos 264-271 from English Electric, had them on the nearside. Many of

the stair risers were fitted with toughened glass to enable the conductor to see the platform from inside the saloon. There were no bulkheads and in the spacious upper saloon the seats were all fitted transversely as in the Rotherham cars. The clear view forward was much appreciated on the ride through Middleton woods.

The cars were the first to be equipped with the electro-magnetic remote control system with 19-notch master controllers of a type later used in Liverpool. The new Maley & Taunton equal-wheel bogies with swing-link axle boxes, giving the smooth running of the swing bolster type without the rolling motion, gave excellent riding at speed. The livery was pale blue with cream bands.

This was, without doubt, one of the finest double-deck tramcar designs ever produced,

Leeds City Transport Nos 256-271
Built: – Loughborough 1935 (256-263); Preston 1935
(264-271)
Length overall: – 35ft 6in
Length over corner posts: – 23ft 6in
Length of platforms: – 3ft 2½in (door width)
Width overall: – 7ft 1¾in
Height to trolley plank: – 15ft 0in
Height inside lower saloon: – 6ft 2in
Height inside upper saloon: – 5ft 10⅝in
Stairs: – Nearside, straight
Seats (lower saloon): – 30 TU 2+2 red hide
Seats (upper saloon): – 40 TU 2+2 red hide
Trucks: – Maley & Taunton swing-link equal wheel bogies;
27in diameter wheels
Motors: – 4 x GEC WT 181A; 40hp
Controllers: – MV Electro-pneumatic
Brakes: – Hand wheel, air wheel and track, rheostatic

No 255, built Loughborough 1933, had an offside staircase, 4 x MV 109 35hp motors, (later GEC WT 28S), and MV OK 42B regenerative controllers (later MV electro-pneumatic).

The 'Pivotal' cars were introduced in 1925 and served Leeds for 30 years or more. No 146 in Lowfields Road shows the truck clearly. Some 97 of the 200 cars were later fitted with P35 trucks. *R. Brook*

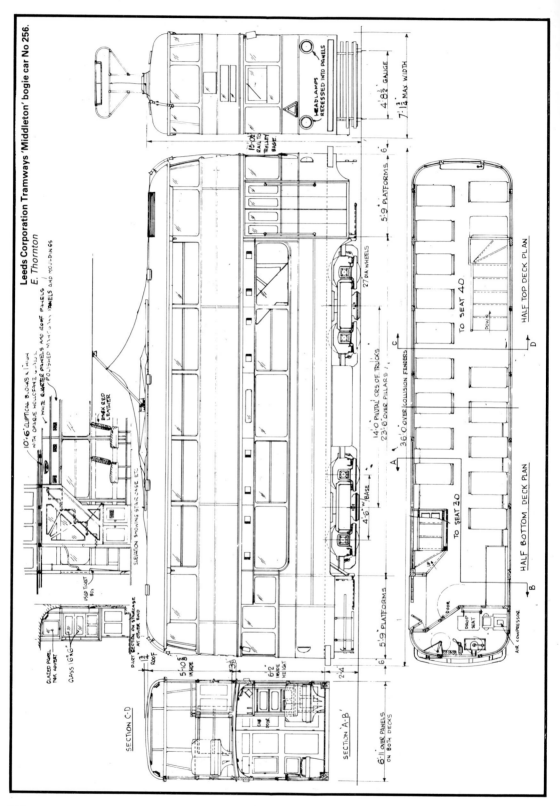

Leeds Corporation Tramways 'Middleton' bogie car No 256.
E. Thornton

The 'Horsfields' of 1931 were solidly constructed and most survived until the end of the tramways in 1959. A new dark red livery with cream bands had been adopted in 1950; No 168 has the standard destination display. Sliding vents were also introduced in upper saloon windows as seen in the interior of No 180.

especially when considered in terms of neatness of line and interior layout. Sadly there were only 17 built and all were scrapped before the preservation movement got into its stride, as were the three single-truck versions to the same general design built at Kirkstall Road between 1933 and 1935. Numbered 272-274, they seated 60 passengers (26+34) with the 'Bucket' seats being particularly comfortable. These cars had Maley & Taunton swing link trucks of 8ft 6in wheelbase but had direct control using old equipment. An austerity version, No 104 (later 275), using a P35 truck, was built in 1943; there was one other, No 276 of better quality and also on a P35, in 1948.

Later rolling stock shortages were made good with second-hand purchases from Hull, London, Manchester and Southampton, and also one single-deck car from Sunderland. This latter vehicle was bought for evaluation in connection with modern tramway developments which included city centre subways, new extensions and single-deck cars.

The Sunderland car was eventually rebuilt and entered service on 4 August 1954 as Leeds No 600, some 14 months after the two new prototype cars, Nos 601 and 602. These two cars had bodies by Charles H. Roe of Cross Gates, Leeds, and were of the company's patented teak and steel composite construction. They had two saloons divided by a central entrance and separate drivers cabs. The interior decor was red and cream with 'Alhambrinal' coverings, and lights were fitted below the longitudinal luggage racks on each side and additionally along the centre line of each saloon.

The cars differed electrically. No 601 had equipment by Metro-Vick and No 602 by Crompton Parkinson. The control equipment was housed above the centre entrance and both cars offered automatic acceleration and braking. No 601 had the

The Middleton bogie was one of the finest tramcars ever built. Its neat lines are apparent in the illustration of No 266, a rush hour extra at Lawnswood in February 1948, which had strayed off the Middleton Light Railway.
E. N. C. Haywood

master controller system but No 602 was all-electric with VAMBAC joystick control, forward for acceleration and back for braking.

They entered service on 1 June 1953 in a livery of Royal purple and cream with gold leaf lines to mark the present Queen's Coronation. It was intended to repaint the cars in standard livery when due for major overhual, but they were withdrawn by 1957, and today No 602, still in the purple livery, is preserved at Crich. It remains as a memento to a tramway scheme that was defeated by lack of finance when municipal transport had to be self-supporting and infrastructure grants were not available.

A through tram service, using cars with trucks adapted for dual gauge working, once linked Leeds with Bradford, and (in passing) the ubiquitous Bradford open-balcony car can surely be regarded as a classic tramcar.

Electric tramway operation in Bradford dates from 29 July 1898 (Yorkshire was early in the field!) and at the peak of expansion 252 cars were, in most cases, climbing the hills that surround the city on three sides. It was these steep gradients that prevented the use of enclosed cars on Bradford's 4ft gauge tracks, and so the open-balcony car became the standard from 1912 onwards as the earlier open-top, short canopy cars from Brush or Milnes were rebuilt or replaced.

Most of the new cars were built at the Thornbury works and from 1919 to 1931 a total of 96 cars were built on traditional lines to this classic design. The distinguishing features of these cars were 'Panelled' hexagonal dashes, square windscreens and four-window saloons with opening lights above. Framed drop windows with fixed lights

Leeds City Transport Nos 601-602

Built: – Cross Gates 1953
Length overall: – 41ft 5¼in
Length over corner posts: – 14ft 10in (each saloon)
Length of platforms: – 4ft 10in
Width overall: – 7ft 3in
Height to trolley plank: – 15ft 0in
Height inside saloon: – 7ft 3in
Seats (each saloon): – 17 TU 2+1 and 6 LU; 36 standing in saloons and platform
Trucks: – EMB lightweight, 5ft wheelbase (601); M&T Type 717 (602)
Motors: – 4 x MV (601); 4 x CP C92 45hp (602)
Controllers: – MV electro-pneumatic (601); VAMBAC (602)
Brakes: – Hand wheel, air wheel and track, magnetic track (601); rheostatic shaft and magnetic track (battery operated) on 602.

were used on the upper decks although some cars of 1928-30 design had plate glass windows. The open balconies were surrounded by decency panels and a wire mesh grill. The livery was latterly light blue and replaced the original Prussian blue with gold lining.

No 104 was built in 1925, withdrawn in 1950, rescued from Odsal stadium by local enthusiasts in 1953 and restored to operational condition in 1958, using equipment obtained from around the country. It now resides at the Bradford Industrial Museum.

**Bradford Corporation Tramways 1924 type double-deck
standard tramcar with Brill 21E wide wing truck.**
E. Thornton

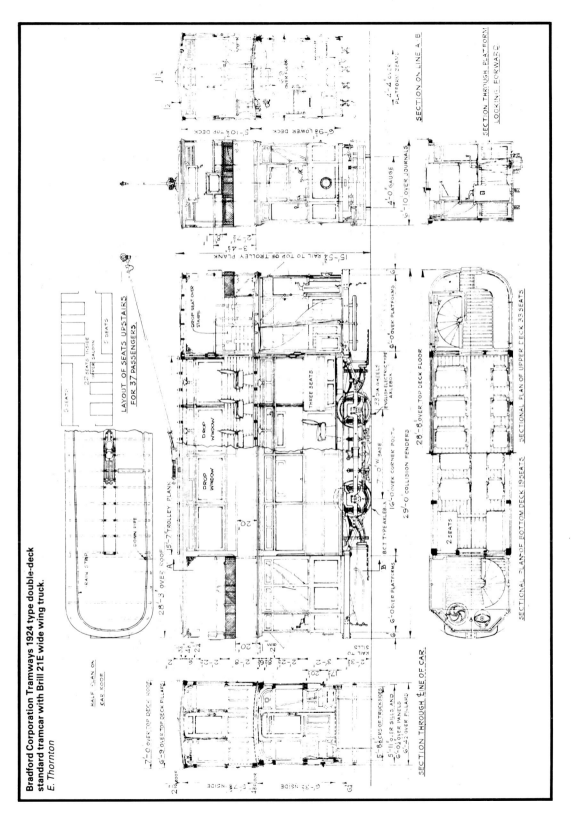

115

Bradford Corporation Tramways No 104
Built: – Thornbury 1925
Length overall: – 29ft 0in
Length over corner posts: – 16ft 0in
Length of platforms: – 6ft 6in (including fenders)
Width overall: – 7ft 0in
Width over corner posts: – 6ft 4½in
Height to trolley plank: – 15ft 5¾in
Height inside lower saloon: – 6ft 3½in
Height inside upper saloon: – 5ft 7⅝in
Stairs: – Direct 180°
Seats (lower saloon): – 19 TU 2+1 moquette
Seats (upper saloon): – 28 TU 2+2 brown leather; and 15 wooden on balconies
Trucks: – DK 21 E ww 7ft wheelbase; (Now Brill 21E ww 6ft wheelbase ex-Sheffield 358)
Motors: – EE DK 31; 60hp
Controllers: – EE DB1 Form K4
Brakes: – Hand wheel and track, rheostatic
Gauge: – 4ft 0in

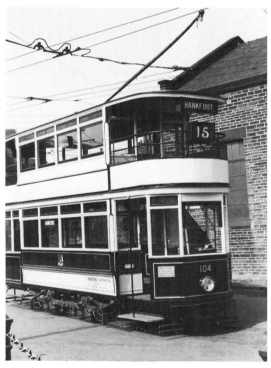

Above:
Of the 90 Felthams purchased only 83 eventually ran in Leeds. Because of their length they were used on east-west services – No 552 is passing the old Corn Exchange loop on 4 October 1953.
Right:
The classic Bradford open-balcony car is represented by No 104 now preserved at the Bradford Industrial Museum. It was photographed at Thornbury in 1958. *J. S. King*

Edinburgh

The City and Royal Burgh of Edinburgh is noted for its wide streets and spacious squares. It has many steep hills, and cable tramcars were introduced in 1888. The Edinburgh & District Tramways Co eventually worked 23.75 miles (38.2km) of route with over 200 cars, operating electric cars on the short Slateford route, with the adjacent Leith Corporation Tramways also electrically operated. The company tramways were taken over by Edinburgh Corporation on 1 July 1919 and those of Leith on 20 November 1920, when the Burghs were amalgamated.

The conversion of the former cable system to electric operation was completed within five years; electric cars started on the Mound and Hanover Street routes on 8 June 1924 although the last cable car had run into Portobello depot a year earlier on 23 June 1923. To operate the new system and the many extensions most of the cable cars were electrically equipped and 240 new cars of traditional design added to the fleet by 1934. These included 138 built at the Shrubhill works of the former company.

Meanwhile moves were afoot to produce a more modern tramcar, and the first break from tradition came in March 1932 when No 180, a new lightweight car in a bright red livery, emerged from Shrubhill to create quite a sensation in the city. Designed by the Transport Department's own engineers, the straight-sided body was built up of

Edinburgh Corporation Tramways No 180
Built: – Edinburgh 1932
Length overall: – 29ft 9in
Length over corner posts: – 17ft 0in
Length of platforms: – 6ft 1in
Width overall: – 7ft 3in
Width over corner posts: – 7ft 3in
Height to trolley plank: – 15ft 9in
Height inside lower saloon: – 6ft 1⅝in
Height inside upper saloon: – 6ft 0³⁄₁₆in
Stairs: – Straight (90° turn at top and bottom)
Seats (lower saloon): – 26 TU 2+2 blue leather
Seats (upper saloon): – 38 TU 2+2 red leather
Trucks: – M&T 8ft 6in wheelbase (initially EMB 8ft 6in)
Motors: – 2 (initially MV 101, 50hp)
Controllers: – MV (later BTH)
Brakes: – EMB (later M&T) air-wheel and track, magnetic track

aluminium alloys on a steel underframe. The first Edinburgh car to have five windows, it also had a flat roof, Ashanco air extractors and enclosed lighting. The extra width in the lower saloon, due to its straight-sided construction, allowed double seats to replace the 2+1 arrangement on the older cars. The seats were upholstered in leather, blue in the lower saloon and red in the upper, with matching rexine on the side panels. An interesting

Standard cars of traditional design for Edinburgh were built at Shrubhill between 1922 and 1934. No 338 of 1925, originally built with open platforms, is seen here passing the Ship Inn at Fisherow.

innovation was the doors on the platform; that to the right shut off the stairs and protected the motorman from draughts, and that on the left the compartments housing the resistance unit at one end and the compressor, etc, at the other.

After three weeks of trials and demonstrations No 180 entered service on 3 April 1932 with an EMB truck, replaced within the week by one of the Maley & Taunton type.

Above:
Quite a sensation when new in 1932, lightweight car No 180 was the first step towards the modern Edinburgh fleet. This photograph of the car was taken near Colinton in 1955.

Below:
All-metal 'streamlined' cars came to Edinburgh during 1934-35. One of the last trams to be built at Motherwell was No 12, seen here on Stanley Road soon after delivery.
The late E. O. Catford, courtesy D. L. G. Hunter

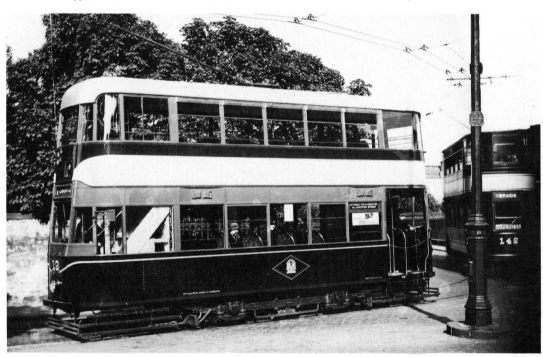

At this time all-metal bus bodies were attracting attention and in 1933 Metropolitan-Cammell supplied two new all-metal cars, Nos 260 and 265. They were generally similar to No 180 except for the flat angular ends which gave them a more traditional look. A further six cars, Nos 241, 242, 244-246 and 249, the first with domed roofs and hence a more modern appearance, followed in 1934, while the three from Hurst Nelson (Nos 231, 239 and 240) had domed roofs and rounded corner panels. These cars all had modern Maley & Taunton 8ft 6in wheelbase trucks.

The last experimental all-metal cars were built by English Electric in 1934 and could easily be distinguished by their down-swept roof ends, and the route lights and indicator box positioned in the panelling between decks, not in the top nearside window which was now too small to hold it. Compared with No 180, Nos 262, 263 and 267 had a slightly tapering upper saloon with domed roof and a marked taper at the ends which reduced their seating capacity by six to 58 (24+34).

A further 20 cars of this type were obtained during 1934-35 from English Electric (Nos 19-24), Metropolitan Cammell (Nos 25-30) and Hurst Nelson (Nos 11-18). Trucks were Nos 262, 263 and 25-30 Maley & Taunton, 267 English Electric, and 11-24 rebuilt Peckham P22s from scrapped cars, some later replaced by a modified Maley & Taunton type.

The 'streamlined' car, however, did not become the new standard for the city; instead the final design was based on No 261, an experimental car of 1933 which was similar to the last traditional cars but had straight sides and hence a higher seating capacity. The '1934' standard cars were developed from this, but had domed roofs, five windows instead of four and an additional single seat opposite the top of the stair at each end.

The cars were of composite construction with aluminium alloy castings in the pillars. The lower saloon main side panels were of plywood sandwiched between aluminium sheets, while the upper saloon panels were similar, but thinner with aluminium sheets on the outside only. The domed roof body had five balanced half-drop windows on each side of the upper saloon and two on each side of the lower, with the frames finished in polished steel. The ceiling consisted of Alhambrinal white aluminium with, on some of the second series of cars, a raised pattern picked out in a darker colour. The car lighting was recessed into the ceiling coves and each fitted with a lampshade that had a quick-fix opening device. The transverse seats, of the usual throw-over type, were, in most cases, of sponge rubber covered with blue leather and moquette in the lower saloon and red leather in the upper (brown in the second series).

The Edinburgh tramcar was designed for rapid loading and unloading, quick acceleration and a

Edinburgh Corporation Tramways No 35
Built: – Edinburgh 1948
Length overall: – 30ft 0in
Length over corner posts: – 17ft 0in
Width overall: – 7ft 3in
Width over corner posts: – 7ft 3in
Height to trolley plank: – 15ft 3¾in
Stairs: – Straight (90° turn at top and bottom)
Seats (lower saloon): – 24 TU 2+2 blue moquette
Seats (upper saloon): – 38 TU 2+2 brown leather
Trucks: – Peckham P22; 8ft 6in wheelbase
Motors: – 2 x MV 101; 50hp
Controllers: – BTH 510A
Brakes: – M&T air-wheel and track, magnetic track

The prototype for the final Edinburgh design was No 261 of 1933. In many ways traditional with ventilating lights and flat roof, it had flush panelling and upholstered seats.
The late E. O. Catford, courtesy D. L. G. Hunter

119

high cruising speed. The platforms were spacious and access to the upper saloon was facilitated by having the staircase located to the front as in car 180. The driver had a portable seat, and a hinged door closed off the stairs. Latterly most Edinburgh cars had two 40 or 50hp motors and Maley & Taunton air-wheel and track brakes, the latter being combined with the magnetic track brake.

A total of 84 cars were built to this final design with the last six appearing in 1950. They were direct replacements for the remaining converted cable cars and incorporated some re-conditioned equipment including the P22 trucks.

The Edinburgh tramcars with their high quality exterior paintwork, restrained streamlined effect and good riding qualities, were well maintained, and one of these classics, No 35, was retained by the city and ran in the Blackpool Centenary procession in 1985.

The production cars with domed roofs and restrained lines were a credit to the city. The lower saloon (*Above left* **) had moquette upholstery and the upper saloon (** *Left* **) leather: note the single seats near the centre to facilitate movement. No 35 (** *Below* **), photographed at Goldenacre in April 1955, ha since been preserved.** *D. L. G. Hunter (2)/R. J. S. Wiseman*

Glasgow

Glasgow Corporation Tramways came second to the London County Council in the number of tramcars operated, and the 'Glasgow Standard' came second only to the 'E/E1' class in London. Part of the Glasgow scene for over half a century, these trams have every right to be included among the classic tramcars. The first prototype appeared in 1898 and the last, No 1088, to the same basic design, in June 1924. Apart from preserved cars the longest lived was No 751 which was built in 1900 and scrapped in 1960.

Electric traction began in Glasgow on the Springburn route on 13 October 1898 with 21 centre-entrance single-deck bogie cars, but with sufficient clearance provided under all bridges in the city the double-deck car won the day for quantity production.

All the standard cars, except Nos 901-980 contracted out to the Gloucester Carriage & Wagon Co, were built at Coplawhill in three main series. The first series of 541 cars built from 1899 to 1901 were open-top short-canopy cars on Brill 21E trucks. They had five 'bow' window saloons with monitor roof and strip or louvre ventilators. They

Glasgow Corporation Tramways 'Standard'
Built: – Coplawhill 1898-1924
Length overall: – 30ft 0in
Length over corner posts: – 17ft 0in
Length of platform: – 6ft 0in
Width overall: – 7ft 3in
Height to trolley plank: – 15ft 17½in
Height inside lower saloon: – 6ft 9in
Height inside upper saloon: – 6ft 6in
Stairs: – Direct 180°
Seats (lower saloon): – 21 TU 2+1 grey moquette
Seats (upper saloon): – 38 TU 2+2 brown leather
Trucks: – Brush 21E 8ft wheelbase 27in diameter wheels
Motors: – 2 x MV, EE or GEC; 60hp
Controllers: – EE CDB2, KC1 or MV OK
Brakes: – Hand, air-wheel track, EMB interlock
Gauge: – 4ft 7¾in

Data for final condition

The Glasgow 'Standard'

The phase I standard car was open-top and the phase II unvestibuled. No 397, the phase III prototype, shows clearly where the vestibule has been added to the phase II car.
Scottish Tramway Museum Society

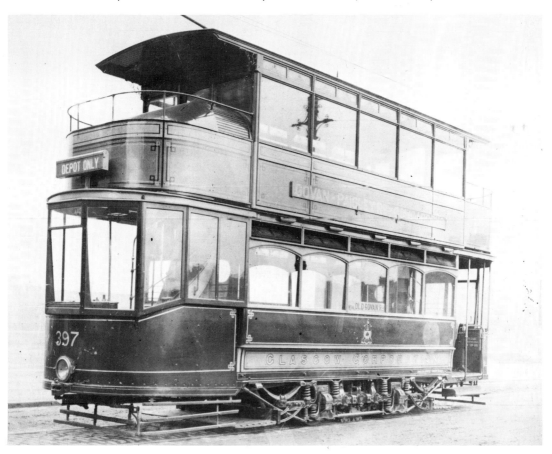

Glasgow Corporation Tramways Phase III Standard car No 22. *I. G. McM Stewart*

No 141, a phase III 'Hex Dash' car as built with open top, with an electrified horse car alongside for road safety purposes. *Scottish Tramway Museum Society*

had normal quarter-turn stairs and low platform dashes. Another 30 open-top cars were built in 1909-10, but these had flat roofs, air scoops and glass ventilators which applied to all standard cars built from 1904 onwards.

After two prototypes, the second series comprised 121 cars built between 1904 and 1910. These were balcony cars with short roofs and half-turn stairs and all of the earlier cars were also given short roof top-covers. The last 20 cars of this series had saloons 4in wider, and this applied to the last series built from 1910 onwards. These cars had hexagonal dashes, vestibuled platforms and open balconies with full-length top-covers.

The 312 cars built to this specification brought the total number up to 1,004, and the 'Glasgow Standard' had a near monopoly of the city streets. Although trams taken over from the Airdrie & Coatbridge Co never penetrated the city streets, ex-Paisley & District Nos 1053-1072 were allocated to city depots for some considerable time.

This construction was not, however, the end of the 'Standard' story. As in other cities there was increasing competition from omnibuses and to combat this there was a massive programme to modernise the tramcars. Virtually all the cars went through the works to emerge over the years 1928-35 as totally enclosed with upholstered seats, improved lighting, airbrakes, new longer wheel-base trucks and 'Fischer' bow collectors.

The progressive modernisation of the 'Standard' shows in its structure. Both saloons were entered through a bulkhead sliding door; the five small windows of the lower saloon gave it a cosy look, warm, muggy and friendly on a wet winter day. Upstairs the windows were rectangular and larger, and the roof structure was clearly seen. The ventilation was through opening lights, but the best way, at least in summer, to clear the tobacco haze was to lower the front canopy window, by pulling up a strap as in old third class railway carriages, and let the wind through as the car sped to the outer terminus. At the same time the conductor could lean out and change the destination screens. The large indicator boxes were outside the balcony panelling; they looked stuck on, as did the vestibules fitted to the older cars. The low dashes dating back to the earliest open-top cars were another distinguishing feature and gave the cars a drooping look.

Lastly, until at least 1938, these cars were among the most colourful in Great Britain, for in addition to the basic livery of orange and cream, the decency panels were painted different colours – red, green,

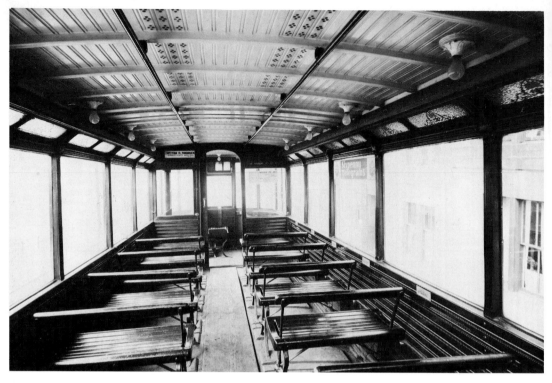

The upper saloon of No 745, with wooden seats, glass ventilators, ribbed ceiling and unshaded bulbs. No 745 was scrapped in this condition, but most standards were fitted with upholstered seats.
Scottish Tramway Museum Society

blue, white or yellow – according to the route operated. In 1938 route numbers were introduced, for the second time, and the various colours gradually gave way to the standard lighter green which was used on the buses.

In its final form the 'Standard' was fast and often furious, especially when behind schedule, and this treatment had a detrimental effect on the bodywork, so much so that most cars had to have the bodies strengthened by ties and bracing; some cars were even braced a second time to keep them on the road until scrapped.

The modernisation programme with hindsight may have been the wrong decision, but at least it kept the 'Standards' going and gave numerous enthusiasts the opportunity to enjoy a unique form of tram travel as late as 1960.

Prior to the start of the modernisation programme two experimental cars had been built; a single-deck high speed car, No 1089, in 1926, and an enclosed double-deck bogie car, No 1090, a year later. The first remained as one only, but 50 new cars of traditional design and similar to No 1090 were built by outside contractors, Hurst Nelson, R.Y. Pickering and Brush. Nos 1091-1140 ran on LCC-type bogies built by the Kilmarnock Engineering Co; the bogies, after problems at city centre junctions, confined them to the Partick-Dalmarnock main line.

During the early 1930s Glasgow was facing the same problems as Liverpool, increasing traffic based on low fares and an increasingly obsolete fleet only kept going by drastic remedial work. The obvious answer was new cars and two prototypes were built at Coplawhill; No 1141 on EMB Lightweight bogies in December 1936 and No 1142, on Maley & Taunton bogies, in March 1937. The latter car had a five-window body and entered service in a striking livery of red, blue and silver grey in honour of the Coronation of King George VI. It was the first Coronation tram.

The production cars were built between November 1937 and July 1940 and took the fleet numbers 1143 to 1292. A further six, Nos 1393-1398, were built in 1954 to a modified design on ex-Liverpool bogies.

The Coronation was a modern tramcar of high quality with a welded steel underframe, substantial bulkheads and composite pillars. The saloons were spacious with four large windows, Alhambrinal panelling and good quality seating. The lower saloon had continuous lighting diffusers which also acted as air ducts for the forced air ventilation. Glass eaves gave extra light to the upper saloon,

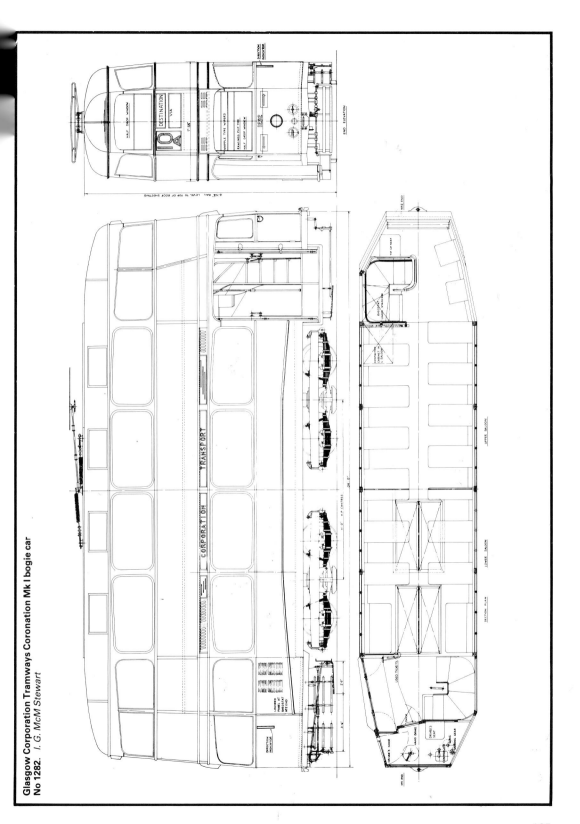

**Glasgow Corporation Tramways Coronation Mk I bogie car
No 1282.** *I. G. McM Stewart*

and ventilation was through half-drop windows at each end. To give the extra length required for the platforms the body tapered inwards from the corner posts. Double folding doors were fitted and the contactor equipment was housed beneath the half turn stairs. Entry to the driver's cab was from the platform or nearside door, but it was rather cramped due to the tapering body ends, even with the smaller master controller.

The Coronations were expensive to build and to operate and so single-truck cars with similar style bodies were built for comparison purposes at Coplawhill in 1939-40. Nos 1001-1004 also served as test pieces for different trucks and equipments, and a fifth car, a new No 6, was built in 1942.

The last experimental car to be built was the single ended No 1005 which made its debut in December 1947. (December was a popular month for new cars, it seems!) This was a further attempt to introduce passenger flow with front entrance and rear exit, but as one car in a fleet of over a thousand with rear entrances, not to mention buses, it was not successful. It was converted to a conventional car in 1951.

A year later came the first Coronation Mk II or Cunarder, of which 100 were built over the years 1948-1952. Nos 1293-1392 resembled No 1005 in body design, which in essence was a simplified version of the Coronation. Modifications included sliding vents in the windows instead of forced air ventilation, concealed lighting in the lower saloon

Glasgow 'Standards' in their final form

Above:

Phase I car No 853 with strip ventilators on Paisley Road West, Crookston, on 15 September 1954.

Glasgow Corporation Tramways, Nos 1141-1292, Coronation Mk 1

Built: – Coplawhill 1936-40
Length overall: – 34ft 0in
Length over corner posts: – 20ft 6in
Length of platforms: – 6ft 6in
Width overall: – 7ft 3½in
Height to trolley plank: – 15ft 5¼in
Height inside lower saloon: – 6ft 3in
Height inside upper saloon: – 5ft 11⅜in
Stairs: – Direct 180°
Seats (lower saloon): – 27 TU 2+2 patterned moquette
Seats (upper saloon): – 38 TU 2+2 green hide
Trucks: – EMB lightweight equal wheel; bogies 4ft 6in wheelbase; 27in diameter wheels*
Motors: – 4 x BTH; 35hp
Controllers: – BTH remote control system
Brakes: – Hand, air wheel/track, electro-magnetic, GCT emergency
Gauge: – 4ft 7¾in

* No 1142 had Maley & Taunton bogies

Glasgow Corporation Tramways, Coronation Mk II Cunarder Nos 1293-1392

Built: – Coplawhill 1948-52
Length overall: – 34ft 6in
Length over corner posts: – 20ft 6in
Length of platforms: – 6ft 9in
Width overall: – 7ft 3½in
Height to trolley plank: – 15ft 3in
Height inside lower saloon: – 6ft 2in
Height inside upper saloon: – 5ft 11in
Stairs: – Direct 180°
Seats (lower saloon): – 26 TU 2+2 patterned moquette*
Seats (upper saloon): – 40 TU 2+2 red leather
Trucks: – Maley & Taunton Type 596 equal wheel; bogies 5ft wheelbase
Motors: – 4 x MV 109; 36hp
Controllers: – MV electro-pneumatic
Brakes: – Hand, Maley & Taunton air, magnetic
Gauge: – 4ft 7¾in

* Early cars up to No 1348 had 30 seats

and jack-knife doors. They had a uniform floor level necessitating three steps up to the platform. This feature, together with a divided entrance, reduced the platform area and caused congestion at busy times.

By now, however, the decline of the Glasgow tramway system had begun, the inter-urban routes to Airdrie and Milngavie had succumbed to the blue trains, trolleybuses had eaten into parts of the urban area and the obsolete tramcars, from 1954 onwards, were being replaced by new diesel buses.

Once started the abandonment programme gathered speed and the last tram ran on 4 September 1962. Fortunately by this time tramcar preservation was a growth industry and no less than 18 tramcars built for Glasgow are still extant in museums.

To travel on a Coronation tram was to travel in comfort and at speed; they could outpace the express buses on the Langloan reserved tracks. It could be argued that they were, like Aberdeen's, too luxurious for urban travel and too expensive when compared with urban buses.

To my mind the Coronation tram was one of the best and superior to its successor, the Cunarder; after all the final double-deck cars to be built had the Coronation style body – and if you're not sure make your own decision by going to Crich where you can still enjoy a little luxury travel on Coronation No 1281 or Cunarder No 1297.

Fleet Lists
Standard cars (as built)
Series I Prototypes: No 686-687
Series I: Nos 688-1000, 665-440, 337
Series II: Nos 439-287
Series III: Nos 286-293, 92-1, 665-685(ii), 987 (ii), 1039-1040, 1051-1052, 1088
Coronation
Nos 1141-1292.
Modified Coronations: Nos 1393-1398
Cunarders
Nos 1293-1392

Phase II car No 298 with opening lights, at Riddrie on 10 August 1955.

Above:
Phase III 'Hex Dash' car No 161, at Commerce Street junction.

Below:
The 'Coronation' was hailed as luxury transport in 1938. No 1290, which entered service in 1940, waits at Rutherglen lights for 'Kilmarnock Bogie' No 1127 to swing round from Glasgow on 4 August 1955.

The luxury of the 'Coronation'

Below:
Prototype car No 1142 had a five-window saloon, but its decor and lighting set the standard for the production cars.
Both Scottish Tramway Museum Society

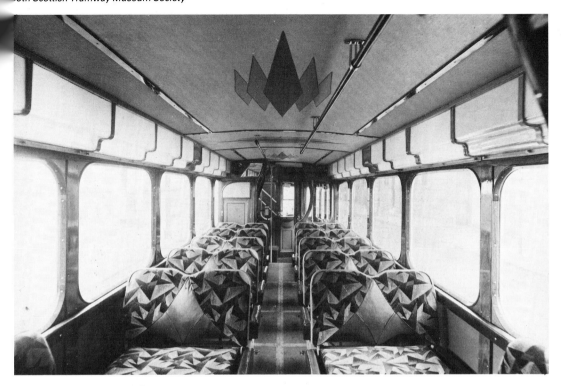

Mark II Coronation or 'Cunarder' No 1298 waits at Riddrie terminus for No 1386 to reverse. Note the modified top window in No 1298 and the contrast with Coronation No 1290.

7. Blackpool

The first electric tramway along the Blackpool Promenade was officially opened on 29 September 1885 with open top double-deck cars operating on the conduit system. The line was constructed by the Corporation and leased to the Blackpool Electric Tramway Co Ltd, for seven years, and when the lease expired on 10 September 1892 Blackpool Corporation took over and became the first municipal authority to operate an electric tramway. The overhead system was adopted in 1899 and the tracks extended into the suburbs. In addition the Blackpool & Fleetwood Co was taken over on 1 January 1920 together with its stock of single-deck cars.

The original cars of 1885 and later were followed in 1898 by the first two 'Dreadnoughts' – real classics! Nos 15-16 with eight side windows were built by Milnes as conduit cars; they were followed

Dreadnought No 59 – the classic Blackpool tramcar seen newly restored in the original red, white and teak livery of 1905. The full-width steps to the platform and the double staircase emphasises the ability of this car to absorb the Promenade crowds.

A busy scene at Fleetwood terminus with two cars in the cream livery with green window frames. *R. Brook*

by Nos 17-26 with six windows in 1900 and Nos 54-61 with five in 1902, all built by the Midland Railway Carriage & Wagon Co Ltd at Shrewsbury. These cars were designed specifically for absorbing the summer crowds on the promenade. They had seats for 86 or 93 passengers and their distinguishing feature, in addition to their size, was the patent double staircase and full-width steps down to the track, at each end of the car.

They were replaced by modern English Electric cars with open tops and seats for 94 passengers in 1934. Fortunately No 59 survived as a tool room in Copse Road depot on the Fleetwood line and was in due course restored for the 75th anniversary celebrations.

While the promenade services called for large double-deck cars, the Fleetwood tramroad, with longer distances between stops and all the year traffic, was best served by single-deck cars.

By 1928 the original company cars were 30 years old and in need of replacement. Ten new vestibuled saloon cars, Nos 167-176, were supplied by English Electric in 1928-29 and worked the North Station-Fleetwood service almost exclusively until the arrival of the first railcoaches in 1935. Officially designated 'Pullman Cars', they were originally fitted with pantographs; the name 'Pantograph' has stuck and is still applied to preserved car No 167.

The cars had flush panelled sides, six-window saloons and clerestory roofs. The 'Pullman' features included transverse upholstered seating,

Blackpool Corporation Tramways No 59

Built: – Shrewsbury 1902
Length overall: – 41ft 0in
Length over corner posts: – 26ft 0in
Width overall: – 7ft 0in
Stairs: 'Shrewsbury' double
Seats (lower saloon): – 44 TW 2+2
Seats (upper saloon): – 49 TW 2+2
Trucks: – Midland RC & W
Motor: – 2 x GE54; 29hp (when built)
Controllers: – BTH B18
Brakes: – Hand wheel, rheostatic

Blackpool Corporation Tramways No 167

Built: – Preston 1928
Length overall: – 40ft 0in
Length over corner posts: – 28ft 0in
Length of platform: – 5ft 6in
Width overall: – 7ft 6in
Seats (saloon): – 44 TU 2+2, plus 2 on each platform
Trucks: – EE McGuire equal wheel; bogies 4ft 1in wheelbase (inner axles driven)
Motors: – 2 x GEC WT28L; 50hp
Controllers: – BTH B 510
Brakes: – Hand wheel, air-wheel, rheostatic

airbrakes (the first in Blackpool) and high speed motors. Platform doors and larger metal windscreens were fitted in 1936-37. Traditional features included red glass ventilating lights and double bulkhead doors to the saloon.

The cars so far discussed were well suited to their specific tasks, but for the mundane tasks of suburban service and day-to-day operation along the Promenade the 'Blackpool Standards' were used.

The history of these cars is complicated and their origin dates back to the 12 open-top Hurst Nelson cars of 1902. The first was built at Rigby Road workshops in 1923 and by 1929 there were 42 cars to this design of which 22 were built new at Rigby Road or Motherwell and 20 were renewals of earlier cars. In addition there were 12 'pseudo Standards' – rebuilds of earlier cars.

The body was of traditional Hurst Nelson design with 'Tudor Arch' windows, open balconies and unvestibuled platforms. An interesting feature is the upper-deck window arrangement on some cars, of two large windows in the centre flanked by two smaller ones on each side. This arises because the balcony bulkheads were set well back and the balconies included one glazed panel. Latterly all were vestibuled, but some retained the open balconies to the end and No 40 is their representative in the Crich fleet. These cars gave yeoman service but by 1960 most had been withdrawn, and with them the classic solidly-built

Blackpool Corporation Tramways No 40
Built: – Blackpool 1926
Length overall: – 33ft 10in
Width overall: – 7ft 2in
Height to trolley plank: – 16ft 2½in
Stairs: – Direct 90°
Seats (lower saloon): – 32 TU and LU
Seats (upper saloon): – 46 TW 2+2
Trucks: – EE McGuire; bogies 4ft 1in wheelbase; 30in diameter wheels
Motors: – 2 x BTH 265C; 35hp (inner axles driven)
Controllers: – BTH B510
Brakes: – Hand wheel, rheostatic

Blackpool Corporation Tramways Nos 284-303
Built: – Loughborough 1937
Length overall: – 42ft 3in
Width overall: – 7ft 6in
Seats (saloon): – 48 TU 2+2 (four emergency seats on the platform were soon removed)
Trucks: – EMB equal bogies; 4ft 3in wheelbase; 27in diameter wheels
Motors: – 2 x CP C162; 57hp
Controllers: – Crompton West CTJ
Brakes: – Hand wheel, EMB air-wheel, rheostatic

Popular for enthusiasts' tours, Nos 41 and 40 at Blundell Street depot in June 1958. No 40, built 'round the corner' in 1926, is now preserved. *R. Brook*

high capacity bogie car, once common throughout Lancashire, had disappeared from the everyday transport scene.

Walter Luff became the Blackpool transport manager in 1933 and inaugurated a five-year plan for tramway modernisation. On the rolling stock side this involved the purchase of 116 new tramcars: 27 double-deck and 89 single-deck. The latter included 65 railcoaches, 45 from English Electric in 1933-35 and 20 from Brush two years later.

Although of generally similar design and layout, the Brush cars were the more attractive. The composite body construction included teak flitched with steel, and steel panelling on an underframe of welded rolled steel sections which incorporated a well for the centre entrance. Air operated sliding doors were fitted and each saloon featured tubular heaters, a sliding roof, glass eaves and panel lighting above the half-drop windows.

Modifications carried out on these cars included the replacement of the original heaters by fan heaters in 1963, the removal of the sliding roofs and air operated doors, and the double destination indicators.

The last prewar design, the English Electric cars of 1939, were re-equipped with VAMBAC control during 1949-50 for the Marton route, which closed in 1962. All were scrapped by 1965 except for No 11 preserved at Carlton Colville.

The 'Coronations' were built by Charles Roberts of Horbury and delivered in 1952-54. At the time of their construction they were the last word in tramcar technology with VAMBAC equipment, electro-pneumatic doors and fluorescent lighting. Unfortunately they were heavy cars with steel panelling and, being unreliable, were expensive to operate. Only No 660 of the original 25 remains in stock.

To take advantage of the economics of one man and trailer operation, 10 of the English Electric railcoaches of 1935 were extensively rebuilt in 1958-61 to tow new trailers built during 1960-61 by Metropolitan Cammell Weymann Ltd of Birmingham. Seven of the trailers now have EEZ6 controllers at one end to allow reversible working. These units have seats for 114:53 in the towing cars, Nos 671-677, and 61 in the trailers, Nos 681-687. Nos 678-680 were not modified in this way and their trailers, Nos 688-690, were withdrawn in 1971. Nos 689-690, sold to GEC Traction in 1981, are to go to the West Yorkshire County Council Museum at Bradford.

The high capacity double-deck cars of 1934-35, now numbered 700-726, are still hard at work during the summer on the promenade. No 725 of this series was rebuilt for one man operation in 1978-1979 and re-entered service as No 761 on 2 July 1979. Aimed, as usual in Blackpool, at maximum carrying capacity with minimum operating costs, the car was rebuilt on the original body frame, suitably modified and still sound. The bodywork includes standard bus components and is of lightweight construction. The car seats 98 (44+54) passengers and is equipped with pantograph current collection.

Although the original EE305 57hp motors have been retained and the bogies rebuilt with metalastic suspension, the 1935 controllers have been replaced. The thyristor control system regulates the traction current to the motors on the 'chopper' principle and operation is through a

The Blackpool railcoaches of 1933 set a new standard in urban transport: Brush car No 287 of 1937 is at Bispham depot in September 1959. *F. P. Groves*

'joystick' – push forward for power and pull back for brake with neutral in the centre position.

About three years later No 714 was rebuilt and re-entered service in 1982 as No 762. This car differs from the previous rebuild in having a central exit, and, although like No 761, the original English Electric motors have been retained, the trucks have been redesigned to give improved riding quality. They are also suitable for the new single-deck cars of which No 641, the prototype car, entered service in 1984, but some years must pass before it can claim to be a classic.

Top:
Ten of the English Electric railcoaches were rebuilt in 1959-61 to tow trailers purchased new from Metropolitan Cammell Weymann Ltd. The scene is Talbot Square.
R. Brook

The new image in double-deck tramcar design

Above and overleaf:
English Electric bogie car No 251 of 1934 (*Above*) has since been rebuilt as No 762 for one-man operation. Designed for the heavy summer holiday traffic it has both centre and end entrances. *R. Brook/Blackpool Transport*

8. Preserved Classics

Having traced the development of the tramcar it is fitting to conclude with a number of cars which have survived the wholesale abandonment process which was completed in Glasgow in September 1962. The cars chosen are or have become classic with the passage of time and illustrate different aspects of the car builders craft.

Leicester No 76 – National Tramway Museum, Crich

This car was built in 1904 and represents the canopied 'Preston' product of the traditional period – 'The Improved Preston Reversed Stairway Type'. As built the car was open-top with the standard three-window saloon of oak and ash with mahogany waist panels and Canary whitewood rocker panels and roof. The saloon floor was of deal and the upper deck in tongue and grooved Baltic pine boards.

All inside wood was finished in natural grain and varnished. Ventilation is through four air scoops and opening lights hinged at the bottom while the seats are slatted with backs of perforated plywood. Extra refinements for Leicester include bevelled plate glass windows, mirrors in the upper panels of the bulkheads which could be tipped inwards to admit fresh air, the city Coat of Arms etched into

Almost completely restored as an open-balcony car of the 1920s, Leicester No 76 stands outside the depot in August 1969. *J. H. Price*

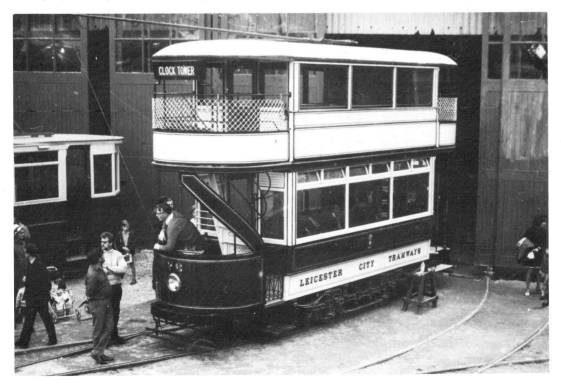

the glass of the saloon door window, and pineapple glass lampshades.

In common with most Leicester cars a rounded roof was fitted, probably in 1920, and in due course No 76 was vestibuled and the balconies enclosed.

After being withdrawn in 1948 and used as a dressing room at East Colwick, the body of No 76 was brought to Crich in 1960. It has since been restored as an open balcony car with equipment from various sources and mounted on the truck from Glasgow No 1017, an ex-Paisley BEC car of 1903.

The restoration programme involved the replacement of the oak cant rail, much of the panelling and the roofing felt. New wire work, made to the original pattern, was fitted round the balconies. The car is finished in the lined out maroon and cream livery which applied prior to 1938.

London County Council Tramways No 106 – National Tramway Museum, Crich

I first saw ex-LCC snowbroom No 022 on 17 November 1956, four years after the closing of London's tramways, in West Norwood depot where it was stored pending rebuilding into LCC Class B car No 106 for the British Transport Collection then at Clapham.

Class B cars were standard Preston products and as delivered were similar in basic structure to Leicester No 76, but were only equipped for conduit operation. They were top covered after a few years, but with the rapid delivery of the new 'E' and 'E1' class cars soon became surplus to normal requirements. All had been sold, scrapped or converted to other uses by 1927, in which year No 106, together with 20 others of the class, was converted into a snowbroom.

As snowbroom No 022 the car survived to the end of tramway operation in 1952 and was put on one side for the BTC Museum. In the event it was donated to the Tramway Museum Society and restored by private donations and much hard work by members of the LCC Tramways Trust.

In common with other rescued cars much of the bodywork had to be replaced, but at least the trucks, motors and controllers had only to be stripped down, repaired where necessary, cleaned and re-assembled.

The saloon interior had the standard 'Preston' ventilation strip above the opening lights and a white painted hardboard ceiling supported by large brackets at each window pillar. The interior trim is entirely of oak with the parts outside the panels stained a darker colour. Most unusually, the panels on the bulkheads and doors do not have bevelled edges but are separated from their surrounds by inlaid beading. The seats are of perforated plywood, and petal lampshades provide a final touch of elegance.

To work the Woolwich-Abbey Wood route on the overhead system, eight 'B' class cars were fitted in 1908 with normal stairs, trolley masts and large destination boxes. No 106, now restored to this condition, and in the crimson lake livery of the LCC Tramways, made its inaugural run at Crich on 15 May 1983 – exactly 80 years after the opening of the LCC electric tramway to Tooting.

Bolton Corporation Tramways No 66

Bolton had a typical South Lancashire system with a fleet of 150 tramcars almost equally divided between bogie and single-truck types. Most of these were built at Preston, including the last traditional enclosed double-deck cars to be built there.

Abandonment of the system began with the Darcy Lever route on 10 March 1928 and was completed with the closure of the Tonge Moor route on 29 March 1947. Some of the redundant car odies ended their days as chalets at a holiday camp near Morecambe while others were dispersed about the local countryside.

When the Bolton enthusiasts started their search for an eight-wheeled tramcar it was almost too late and only the lower saloon of No 66, by then a chicken coop, remained in reasonable condition. It was rescued from its farmyard home in 1963 and nearly 20 years were to pass before it ran again in public service, on 5 July 1981, in Blackpool.

No 66, one of 22 cars (Nos 60-81), was delivered from Preston in August 1901 and was open-top with platform vestibules and reversed stairs. An eight-window open-balcony top-cover was fitted, and the vestibules removed, within a few years, and it was rebuilt again about 1930 with an enclosed top deck and normal-turn staircases.

The Bolton 66 Tramcar Trust, like many other groups, has achieved the near impossible; it has re-created the typical double-deck bogie tramcar from one lower saloon, odds and ends from other bodies scattered around the Bolton area and a new top deck built by a local undertaker – Shaws Woodworking Specialists, cabinet makers, etc. A pair of 22E type bogies was acquired from the Schepdaal Tramway Museum, Belgium and motors from the Stanton Ironworks in Derbyshire. As a result of all the Trust's efforts and an agreement with the Blackpool Borough Transport Department, a whole new generation of holidaymakers are now able to ride in the polished wooden splendour of the traditional tramcar.

Newcaslte Corporation Tramways No 102 – National Tramway Museum, Crich

Electric tramway operation in Newcastle-upon-Tyne opened on 16 December 1901 with 80 single-deck and 20 double-deck cars from Hurst Nelson of Motherwell. In addition the Corporation purchased 30 single-deck open-sided car bodies, eight for single trucks from Brush and 22 for bogies from Hurst Nelson. These were for use during the summer months, but the need for glazed all weather cars was so urgent that it is possible that only one of these cars ran as built.

The bogie cars, Nos 81-110, were dramatically rebuilt at the Byker works during 1903-06. Although three of these Class F cars were fitted with top-covers (one of these later reverted back to open-top), and six were rebuilt with balconies, vestibules and front exits, the majority, including No 102, were uncanopied open-top cars with 12 window saloons and ventilating lights above. Braking of these heavy cars proved a problem, and to improve this No 102 and some others were equipped with airbrakes. These cars were therefore in general, restricted to those routes without significant gradients and were at their best serving Gosforth Park on racedays and the Town Moor on fair days, when their high seating capacity would be fully utilised.

No 102 was withdrawn from service in February 1949 and left Byker depot in April 1950 for Hodgson's Garage, Benton where it was stored on the land free of charge until 9 July 1954. There then followed a return trip to the Montague Motor Museum at Beaulieu, outward via Bury, and it was back at Byker in 1967 for rebuilding – literally! Exposure to the elements for over 10 years had reduced much of the woodwork to pulp.

After eight years of effort, rebuilding was completed (the last stages at Clay Cross), and the car entered passenger service again on the Crich Tramway on 21 July 1975. The interesting features of this car, in addition to its size, are the slatted wooden seats, the plank ceiling and the 'Tudor Arch' bulkheads. The latter proclaim its Hurst Nelson ancestry.

F for Fleetwood in 1984 – Bolton No 66 rounds the corner en route for Fleetwood Ferry; it is showing the appropriate route letter – used for Farnworth on its home system.
G. B. Claydon

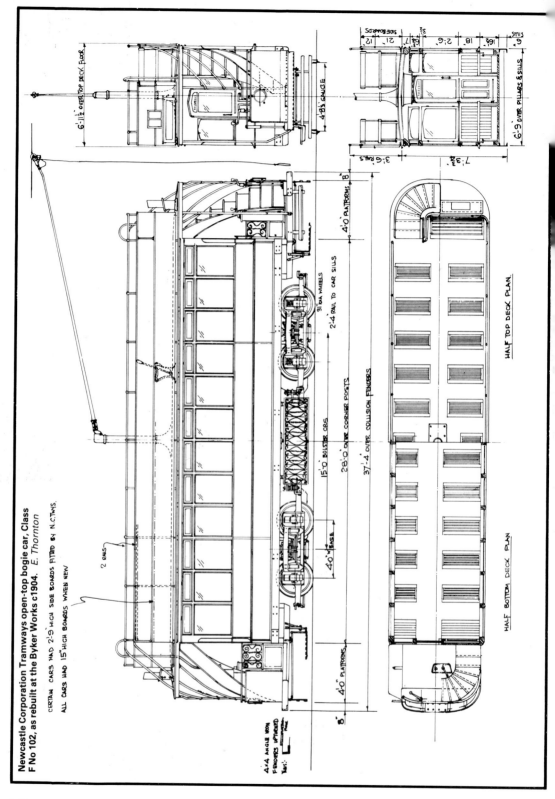

Newcastle Corporation Tramways open-top bogie car, Class F No 102, as rebuilt at the Byker Works c1904. *E. Thornton*

CERTAIN CARS HAD 2'9" HIGH SIDE BOARDS FITTED BY N.C.TWYS.

ALL CARS HAD 15" HIGH BOARDS WHEN NEW

2 RODS

4"x4" ANGLE IRON FENDERS ATTACHED HERE

6'-1½" OVER TOP DECK FLOOR

4'-8½" GAUGE

8"

4'-0 PLATFORMS

31" DIA WHEELS

2'-4" RAIL TO CAR SILLS

15'-0 BOLSTER C&S

28'-0 OVER CORNER POSTS

37'-4" OVER COLLISION FENDERS

4'-0 BASE

4'-0 PLATFORMS

8"

SIDEBOARDS

2'-6"

6'-9 OVER PILLARS & SILLS

3'-6 RAILS

7'-3¾"

HALF TOP DECK PLAN

HALF BOTTOM DECK PLAN

140

Newcastle No 102 on the scrap lines in Gosforth Park. Unlike the other trams in the picture it returned to Byker depot and after many miles across country on low-loaders has reached the National Tramway Museum at Crich. *G. S. Hearse*

Gateshead & District Tramways Co No 5 – National Tramway Museum, Crich

The Gateshead & District Tramways Co was the first of the companies under the BET umbrella to operate electric tramcars, the last official car, No 16, returning to Sunderland Road depot on 4 August 1951. Unlike for most BET companies the initial rolling stock had been purchased from the Electric Railway & Tramway Carriage Works at Preston during 1901-02 (Nos, 1-20 single-deck; Nos 21-45 open-top double-deck) and from the Milnes, Hadley, works (Nos 45-50 single-deck).

In conjunction with through running over the two Tyne bridges into Newcastle, new single-deck bogie cars, Nos 1-20 and 56-60, replaced the older stock during the years 1926-28, Nos 1, 10 and 56-60 being built at Loughborough and the rest at the company's Sunderland Road workshops. (Nos 12, 13, 15 and 19 had detail difference).

No 5 entered service on 10 December 1927 and the new design incorporated a number of features from the Tividale cars. There are no bulkheads but the two four-window saloons are divided by a solid central bulkhead with glazed upper sections. One of these was used to display the fare tables. The car has a clerestory roof but it is hidden from view by

Gateshead & District Tramways Co No 5
Built: – Gateshead 1927
Length overall: – 42ft 8in
Length over corner posts: – 30ft 8in
Length of platform: – 5ft 6in
Width overall: – 6ft 10in
Width over corner posts: – 6ft 10in
Height to trolley plank: – 11ft 3in
Height inside lower saloon: – 7ft 8in
Seats: – 48 LW in two saloons
Trucks: – Brill 39E Rev MaxT; bogies 4ft wheelbase; 32in and 22in diameter wheels
Motors: – 2 x DK31A; 30hp
Controllers: – DB1 K3C
Brakes: – Hand wheel, air wheel and track

advertisement boards. Although built in 1927 each saloon still retains an air of Edwardian solidarity with varnished woods, red roof lights, slatted longitudinal seats and two three-light chandeliers with fancy shades.

These high capacity cars operated on the through service between Gosforth and Lowfell and were built for front exit operation, as were the Newcastle cars used on the same service. Passengers entered at the rear through a sliding

Gateshead No 5 came to Crich via the Grimsby & Immingham Electric Railway. It is seen outward bound on the main line in April 1968. *H. Price*

141

door and left by a hinged door under the control of the motorman.

Fourteen of the cars were sold to the Grimsby & Immingham line of British Railways and operated there until its closure on 4 June 1961. Two cars survive: No 5 at Crich and No 10 at the North of England Open Air Museum at Beamish.

Paisley District Tramways Co No 68 – Nation[al] Tramway Museum, Crich

This car is worthy of inclusion because it was bu[ilt] by Hurst Nelson to the LCC 'M' class design. Th[e] 100 top-covered 'B' class cars were delivered [to] London in 1912-13, but the open-top Paisley car[s] were not delivered until 1916, (Nos 63-67) and 191[7]

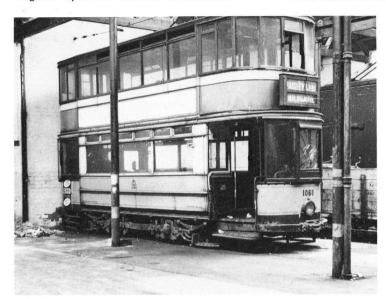

London and Glasgow separated by direct stairs! Paisley No 68 as Glasgow No 1068 photographed in Dalmarnock depot in 1958. Paisley Nos 63-72 had LCC 'M' class three-window lower saloons and open tops, to which Glasgow added its standard four-window upper saloons in 1924. Now restored to its original open top condition, No 68 operates at the Crich museum.

Nos 68-72), and were probably the last open-top cars to be built at Motherwell.

The Paisley cars passed to the Glasgow Corporation Tramways on 1 August 1923 and, renumbered 1063-1072, were fitted with Glasgow standard top covers to produce true hybrids, having LCC 'M' class three-window saloons and Glasgow five-window top decks! In this state they could be said to have recreated systems over 400 miles apart.

No 68 was set aside for the Scottish Tramway Museum Society and came to Crich on 2 September 1960. It has recently been restored under the job creation scheme and now operates as an open-top car in the red and off-white livery of the Paisley District. It exhibits many LCC features, in particular the double corner posts, plank ceiling, slatted longitudinal seats and ventilation lights opened by a centre ratchet mechanism.

Southampton Corporation Tramways No 45 – National Tramway Museum, Crich

Visiting Southampton in October 1944 I arrived at Shirley depot and was invited inside to inspect the rolling stock which included open top cars Nos 39 and 43, the former uncanopied and the latter canopied. These were the first I had ever seen with 'knifeboard' seating along the top deck, so designed to allow passage under the medieval Bargate in the High Street.

Hurst Nelson supplied 12 uncanopied cars in 1903 (Nos 38-49) which in the course of time were rebuilt at the Portswood overhaul works. No 45 finally emerged as a four-window, canopied, but unvestibuled, tramcar. The interior is a fine example of the body-builders craft with its ribbed roof, slatted longitudinal seating and mirrors on each side of the bulkhead doors.

No 45 was the first car to pass into private preservation and, repainted and on an overhauled 21E truck, left Southampton in January 1949. Like Newcastle No 102 it was stored around the countryside until it eventually arrived at Crich on 29 October 1960.

Since that time the car has had considerable attention: panels have been replaced, the interior renovated and all the electrics overhauled, and, as befits the first car to be preserved by an enthusiast group, it heads the procession of tramcars which is a feature at the National Tramway Museum from time to time.

This completes the survey of preserved classics. They have been chosen because they illustrate not only the body-builders craft but also the magnitude of the tasks undertaken by the various preservation groups. Four of the seven cars discussed above were purchased or presented as in running order, but such are the ravages of time and weather that they have had to be overhauled and repainted at least once. The other three cars illustrate what can be achieved by enthusiasm and determination; No 106 was taken over as a snowbroom but complete with truck and equipment; No 76 as a more or less complete body; while of No 66 only the lower saloon was left.

In addition to those listed above there have been many other restoration projects which have been brought to a successful conclusion, including No 5 of the erstwhile Dudley, Stourbridge & District Traction Co. A standard Tividale product of 1920, the body survived for nearly half a century near Dudley. It now operates on the tramway at the Black Country Museum on a 21E type truck from Brussels with controllers from a Grimsby & Immingham car.

The story of the classic tramcar is not yet ended, for in many parts of the country including London, Birmingham, Southampton, Southport and Lowestoft, the rebuilding of once-abandoned tramcars is continuing.

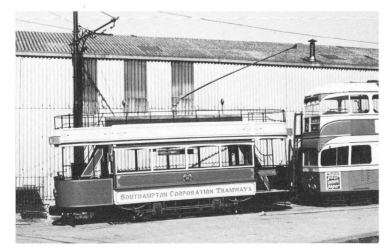

Southampton No 45's new paintwork reflects the sunshine of Crich in May 1984.

Bibliography

Black Country Tramways (2 vols), J.S. Webb; Author 1974, 1976.

The Tramways of Croydon, (revised edition) G.E. Baddeley; LRTA 1983.

Edinburgh's Transport, D.L.G. Hunter; Advertiser Press 1964.

The Tramways of Gateshead, G.S. Hearse; Author 1965.

The Glasgow Tramcar, Ian Stewart; Scottish Tramway Museum Society 1983.

Huddersfield Corporation Tramways, Roy Brook; Author 1983.

The Tramways of Kent (2 vols) 'Invicta' LRTA 1971, 1975.

Liverpool Transport (Vol II), J.B. Horne & T.B. Maund; LRTA/Transport Publishing Co 1983.

Liverpool Corporation Tramways 1937-57, T.J. Martin; Merseyside Tramway Preservation Society 1972-73.

The London Tramcar, R.W. Kinder; The Oakwood Press 1951.

London's Trams & Trolleybuses, J.R. Day; London Regional Transport 1977.

The Manchester Tram, Ian Yearsley; Advertiser Press 1962

The Metropolitan Electric Tramways (Vol I), *C.S. Smeeton; TLRS/LRTA 1984*

The Tramways of Northumberland, G.S. Hearse; Author 1961

The Tramways of Portsmouth, S.E. Harrison; LRTA 1955

Scottish Tramway Fleets, A.W. Brotchie; NB Traction 1968.

The Tramways of Sunderland, S.A. Staddon; Advertiser Press 1964.

Tramcars, J.H. Price; Veteran & Vintage Series; Ian Allan Ltd 1963.

A Source Book of Trams, J.H. Price; Ward Lock 1980.

The Tramways of the West of England, P.W. Gentry; LRTA 1952.

The British Electric Car Company Ltd, J.H. Price; Nemo 1978.

The Brush Electrical Engineering Company Ltd, J.H. Price; TLRS 1976

Hurst Nelson Tramcars, J.H. Price; Nemo 1960.

Great British Tramway Networks (4th edition), W.H. Bett and J.C. Gillham; LRTA 1962.

The Tramways of the East Midlands; The Tramways of South Yorkshire and Humberside; The Tramways of South East Lancashire; The Tramways of North East England; The Tramways of East Anglia; and *The Tramways of North Lancashire* – all adapted from Great British Tramway Networks and edited by J.H. Price.

Modern Tramway – especially 'Birmingham Corporation Tramway Rolling Stock' by P.W. Lawson,'Leeds Trams 1932-59' by A.D. Young, and 'Liverpool Tramways 1943 to 1957' by R.E. Blackburn.

Tramway Review – especially 'The Tramways of Teesside' by G.S. Hearse, 'A History of Oldham's Tramways' by G.G. Hilditch, 'Belfast Corporation Tramways 1905-1954' by J.M. Maybin, 'Cardiff's Electric Tramways' by H.B. Priestley, 'The Tramways of Preston' by G.W. Heywood, 'A History of the Barnsley, Dearne, Mexborough & Rotherham Tramway Conurbation' by C.C. Hall, 'The Douglas Southern' by F.K. Pearson and 'Raworth's Regenerative Demi-cars' by Ian Yearsley.

The files of *Modern Transport* and *Passenger Transport Journal (The Electric Railway, Bus and Tram Journal)* in the Ian Allan Library were also consulted.

LRTA – Light Rail Transit Association
TLRS – Tramway & Light Railway Society